Online

Everyone

How to stay safe on the Internet and protect your personal information without being (too) paranoid

By Evan Anthony

Security is always excessive until it's not enough.
– Robbie Sinclair, Head of Security, NSW Australia

In the digital era, privacy must be a priority.
Is it just me, or is secret blanket surveillance obscenely outrageous?
– Al Gore

Privacy is not an option, and it shouldn't be the price we accept for just getting on the Internet.
– Gary Kovacs

The user's going to pick dancing pigs over security every time.
– Bruce Schneier

Even if you're not doing anything wrong, you are being watched and recorded.

--- Edward Snowden

Relying on the government to protect your privacy is like
asking a peeping tom to install your window blinds.
– John Perry Barlow

Table of Contents

Online Security for Everyone

How to stay safe and protect your personal
information without being (too) paranoid

Chapter 1. Why online security and privacy is important

If you took the time to obtain a book about online
privacy then you no doubt feel that it is an important
topic and that I do not need to convince you any
further. That being said, I will attempt to do so
anyway.

Facts

Fact #1: We spend more time online and conduct more transactions online each year. This means that we also have more and more personal information stored on the Internet every day.

Think of all the types of transactions you do online during the course of the year and then consider the information provided to perform these transactions:

Banking and Financial

Tax returns

Medical claims

DNA results

Shopping at large vendors (Walmart, Amazon, eBay) and also smaller local establishments

Ordering transportation (Uber, Lyft, etc.)

Planning trips (airlines, hotels, cruise packages)

Ordering groceries and food (delivery anyone?)

Government forms related to Social Security, Medicare, passports, etc.

Maps and GPS directions

Email

News feeds, blogs read, and comments and reviews submitted

Videos watched (YouTube, Netflix, Vudu, etc.)

Social network posts

Each of these transactions, at a minimum, include our login information and some basic personal information such as name and email and/or phone number. Some of them contain very sensitive data including SSN, medical history, banking numbers, credit card information, and personal preferences. Social media accounts, of course, contain a plethora of personal information -- that we willingly share-- such as photos, people we know, where we went to school, where we live, our pets' names and of course, what we ate for dinner the last three nights.

All of our data, both sensitive and innocuous, are stored by these online companies. Some of these companies are large and have dedicated IT staff engaged in data security. We will see later that this does not matter as they are still routinely hacked since they are such large targets. Other organizations are small, like your local doctor's office or that pizza place you like to order from, and have essentially no security other than what comes "out-of-the-box" with whichever services they subscribe to.

Fact #2: Online companies are very poor stewards of our personal information.

Why is this the case? There are many reasons but the key points are:

> There is very little legal incentive to protect customer's data, at least in the USA. Europe has the GDPR in place and companies can be

fined heavily for losing sensitive data. In the US you have to prove that you incurred a personal loss (money or otherwise) and it is directly related to the hack in question. This means that it would be almost impossible to sue Equifax (for example) after losing millions of people's credit information. There are a few data protection laws in place, Sarbanes-Oxley and HIPAA to name two, but we will see that this has not prevented data from being stolen and resold on the internet.

There is a lucrative aftermarket for aggregate data to be used in marketing and advertising both online and off. Many companies sell their user data to marketing companies and make a nice extra paycheck. In some cases, the entire business model is gathering data to resell it. Ever use one of those 'find someone online' sites? Ever use Facebook?

Those companies that do not partake in selling data (e.g. your doctor's office) are still vulnerable to data breaches because they do not have IT staff to ensure current security practices.

Why are so many people after your data?
The legitimate (or should I say legal) actors want your data for one main reason -- to sell you stuff. They want your business, and they pay money to try

and target those people who are high percentage potential customers. Since every lead costs money, the higher the conversion rate the more profit a company can make. Maybe they are looking for males under 40 who recently took an international trip, make more than $100,000, and have a dog. This information can be bought. You may not think this is a big deal, in fact you may even like being catered to with products and services that you would not have known about otherwise. However, not everyone is playing by the book.

Unscrupulous persons and downright thieves are online making a lucrative living, without even leaving their homes, or maybe the downtown cafe. They want access to your accounts so that they can impersonate you, steal your identity, and occasionally just mess with you because they can. Mostly, they are trying to steal information which can be resold on the dark web, or trying to steal money. This money can take the form of credit card information, bitcoin, or actual money from your bank account. There have also been scams where they steal social security checks, tax refunds, and mortgage or rent payments.

There is also the admittedly rare case, where someone is spying on you and wants access to your accounts. Maybe you are under surveillance by a private investigator, or you are friends with someone who (unknown to you) is being watched by the FBI, or maybe you are part of an activist group that the local authorities are tracking. Although this is an unlikely scenario for most of you, prudent online security measures will still help keep your data private.

So knowing that your online information is valuable to many people why should you put in effort to protect it? From a privacy standpoint, with net neutrality repealed (in the USA) your ISP and other businesses will be doubling their efforts to collect and act upon more data than ever. From a security standpoint, as described below there are frequent data breaches, and numerous scams and social engineering schemes in which your data can be compromised. Setting up protective walls (e.g. not re-using passwords) and procedures will ensure that the damage will be minimized.

Breaches

Data breaches occur every week in companies large and small. In the past there were many that went unreported, however, now companies are obligated to report when a data breach occurs. You can find a running list of breaches on Wikipedia at https://en.wikipedia.org/wiki/List_of_data_breaches. These data breaches are far-reaching and it is safe to say that at this point everyone in the USA has had some data stolen. According to Wikipedia: in 2019, a collection of 2.7 billion identity records, consisting of 774 million unique email addresses and 21 million unique passwords, was posted on the web for sale. This even includes your 97-year old grandma who has never been online, because she shops for knick-knacks at Target and her credit card number was stolen after hackers got into their network via the heating and air-conditioning network connection (yes, seriously).

Here is a brief overview of some of the bigger data hacks in the past few years:

2019

> Capital One over 106 million records were exposed including information that it routinely collects during credit card applications from consumers and small businesses, including names, addresses, ZIP codes, phone numbers, email addresses, birthdates and reported income.

> DoorDash had over 4.9 million user records breached which includes home delivery addresses.

> American Medical Collection Agency (AMCA) collects overdue payments for medical labs such as Quest Diagnostics, LabCore, CareCentrix, and Conduent. AMCA exposed more than 20 million records of these labs' customers, including sensitive information like Social

Security numbers and bank account information.

First American Financial exposed more than 885 million files related to mortgage deals

Facebook had over 750 million user records breached in 3 separate incidents this year alone.

T-Mobile reported more than one million customers' personal data were exposed to a malicious actor.

Adobe had 7.5 million user records hacked due to poor security.

Unnamed Company - Over 752,000 birth certificate applications have been exposed online by an unnamed company that enables people to obtain copies of birth and death records from state governments in the United States

2018

Marriott International (mostly Starwood, Westin, and Sheraton properties) lost personal and credit card data of over 500 million people from around the world.

The US Postal Service lost personal data of over 60 million American citizens and residents.

Facebook hackers made off with information about 50 million users of the platform.

2017

Equifax hackers gained access to over 143 million people's credit information. This is a company that collects data about you, without your permission, with no choice to opt-out, and then loses that data due to poor security practices.

2016

Hackers obtained access to the IRS and stole information on hundreds of thousands of taxpayers including social security numbers, annual earnings, and home address.

AdultFriendFinder got hacked and over 412 million accounts including profiles, photos, contact information, and a long list of information that could be rather embarrassing was stolen.

Over 1.5 million accounts at Verizon Communications had information stolen.

The US Department of Homeland Security had information from over 30,000 accounts hacked. I find it ironic that the US Government security department had poor security practices.

Just to pound it home a bit more, here are a few more of the biggest hacks in history with account loses in the millions. Have you ever had any transactions with these companies, either via credit card or online account?

Yahoo
eBay
Target
JP Morgan Chase
Home Depot
Gmail
Michael's stores
Neiman Marcus
Uber
Ancestry.com and MyHeritage.com

Hopefully I have convinced you that remaining safe online and keeping your data out of the hands of those who shouldn't have it is worth the effort in time investment. In this day and age it is not possible to "go dark" and stay off the internet -- it's just not realistic. But that doesn't mean you have to surf around with your digital wallet or passport above your head and say "come and get it!" Similarly to personal safety, staying safe online is making yourself less of a target or making it difficult enough to get to your information that they will pass you up for easier targets.

With that in mind, there are two aspects of online security that will be addressed in this book:

- protecting access to your accounts;

- protecting access to your data and personal information stored by 3rd parties

This book focuses mainly on computing devices (Windows and MacOS), but most of the principles can be applied to cell phones as well. There will be another edition of this book specifically for cell phones. I did not want to put all this information in one volume and overwhelm you with security "to-do" items. While there are a lot of suggestions in this book, and a lot of information, do not feel that you have to do all of it, especially all at once. You should consider where you are most vulnerable based on what you do online. This will become clearer as you progress through the chapters.

A Word to Small Business

If you own a small business you may feel that you are too small to be of interest to hackers. This is not true. While you may not have thousands of employees, the data you have is still valuable on the dark web, or if your data gets ransomed for cryptocurrency.

Here are some common information that hackers look to steal from businesses:

Customer credit card and address information
Financial records and banking information
Confidential information and intellectual property

Employee information
Account logins and passwords

According to Experian, the average value for information on the dark web is enough for even an amateur hacker who gets a couple of dozen employees' credentials and personal information to make a nice living.

Here are some recent values for buying stolen information online. Prices are for one record:

Social Security Number $1

Drivers License $20

Credit card number with CVV $5

Subscription service account logins (e.g. Netflix) $5

Medical records $1 - $1000

Online banking and payment account $20 - $200

Passport $1000

Small business are easy targets to hackers because unlike a big corporation which has many walls and gates to get through, a small business typically lacks the budget, the time or staff, and more often than not, their employees are not trained to identify security issues. The effects of a cyberattack or security breach can be severe.

What are some negative aspects of having your network and data hacked as a small business?

    Loss of data
    Downtime
    Damage to reputation
    Regulatory fines or lawsuits
    Loss of productivity
    Identify theft for one or more people
    Loss of money/theft

How long could you remain profitable if you lost access to your data? If this worries you --and it should-- simply read on and implement as many of the recommendations in this book that make sense.

Keep in mind that there is no such thing as perfect security or guaranteed privacy online since, as you can see from the list above, many of these breaches are out of our control unless we live in a cabin in the woods with no communications and use cash everywhere. Even then, your data could be stolen from a hospital, school, or the Government itself.

So let's dive right in and get ready to put on our multi-layer protective armor against all those online dragons.

Chapter 2. Protecting Access to Your Accounts

The first thing that probably comes to your mind when someone mentions online privacy or security is a hacker trying to gain access to your accounts. This could be your email, social media, or banking sites. Your first order of business is to ensure that you protect all of your important accounts from someone gaining easy access. You may not think you have any state secrets in your email account, but with access to your main email, hackers can likely reset passwords to many of your other logins, including your financial accounts. They can also communicate with your contacts and friends posing as you, and thereby compromise their security as well. If they gain access to your social media imagine the havoc and embarrassment that could be caused -- most likely before you even know what happened.

The two common methods for securing access to your online accounts are: passwords; and two factor authentication (2FA).

Passwords

As soon as the word *password* is mentioned, whether at work, home, or a fancy cocktail party, an audible groan can typically be heard. Changing them is one of those things that we all know but just don't do. We all know to be healthy we should eat better, exercise more, drink water, and get 8 hours of sleep. Similarly, we all know that we should avoid reusing passwords, avoid simple or guessable and commonly used words and phrases. But everyone does it at some point. Why? Because memorizing dozens of long and complicated character sequences does not seem to be a good use of our mental capacity; after all we could use that space to store important information like the lyrics to the Jetson theme song or the number of home runs that Derek Jeter hit in his rookie year (i.e. 10).

So is there a better way? The answer is Yes. I will show you several good methods, but first let's look at some important facts on cracking passwords.

How long does it take to crack a password?

As you read in the previous chapter, there are many data breaches each month that include hashed passwords. These files containing passwords are entered into an offline fast-processing servers. So if some irate teenager (aka script-kiddie) or nefarious dark web hacker looking to make some extra money wanted to crack these passwords, how long would it take? Well if you use one of the more common passwords (I'm looking at you 'Football'), or a word that appears in the dictionary, the answer is only a few seconds. Yup, that's all. A password with a length of 6 characters including a symbol generally takes 2.3 seconds, an 8 character password with a symbol about 1.2 minutes; and 10 characters with a symbol and a number is between 2 and 9 months.

So what can we learn from this? Length matters.

If you weren't sure before, now you know. This is bad news for all of you with just 5 or 6 characters -- but luckily you can change this easily and be a password stud. If you do nothing else, use a longer password, a minimum of 10 characters, and if you can get to 15 or 20 your password is statistically uncrackable with today's technology.

Using a number and symbol will help avoid dictionary-related attacks and most websites will now require a number and symbol anyway. So here is a good method for password creation: use passphrases instead of passwords. They are long and easy to remember. You will likely have to come up with a standard substitution such as the first vowel will get replaced with a number and you will always end with a $ symbol (for example). You can use phrases from songs, movies, books, television, or even better just a quote you like or made up.

Here is an example or three:
Every1WangChungTonight! or
ItWasTheBest0fTimes$ or
JennyIveGotYour#8675309.

As you can see, these are easy to remember (if you are a Gen X'er) and are long enough to not worry about brute force password attacks if your account does get caught in a data breach. However, you still should not reuse these passwords since if it gets compromised it can result in gaining access to multiple sites. So what else can be done? Let's talk about password managers...hey, wake up this is important!

Side Notes:

If you have a "favorite" password and want to see how long it would take to crack, go to https://www.grc.com/haystack.htm and enter it and look at the Offline Fast Attack Scenario results.

Here is a list of the most common passwords from the past few years: https://en.wikipedia.org/wiki/List_of_the_most_common_passwords

Password managers

Even if you use the method I described above regarding passphrases it can still be difficult to remember which awesome phrase you used for which site. Or maybe you're sold on the random character password thing, which is just fine and very effective. The best bet for everyone is to download and use a password manager. The most common ones are LastPass, DashLane, BitWarden and 1Password. All of these have free versions that allow password storing, password generation, and synchronizing passwords to the cloud and storing them with strong encryption. All have associated apps for your mobile phone as well.

The one lynchpin for these software apps is that there is a master password that prevents access to **all your other passwords**. So obviously you are going to use a long and complex password here. The passphrase method from above is a good choice here since it should be sufficiently long and you do not want to lose it otherwise you will lose access to your other passwords. Under no circumstances should you use a simple or easy to determine password for your password manager.

I recommend BitWarden. This application is 100% open source software. That means the code can be examined and reviewed by anyone to ensure there is no funny business going on. It has received a thorough security assessment and cryptographic analysis by a third-party security auditing firm. Like the others, there is a free version – which should be sufficient for all personal use – and a paid version aimed at businesses. It runs on almost every browser, and all 3 major operating systems. There is a cell phone app for both Android and iPhone.

As a point of note, some people state that using a cloud password manager like those listed above is still risky in that if the site is compromised that you could lose all of your passwords at once. Again, if you protect this account with a very good password the hashing algorithm used by these sites presents a minimal risk that this could happen since the data is encrypted on their server. However, if you prefer to keep everything local, you can look at KeePass password manager. It is free and does a great job. I will admit that you need to be a bit more technically inclined to use it however. The cloud solutions are just so much more convenient for not much risk, and a whole lot more user-friendly. But you can choose what is best for you.

So what are the advantages of using a cloud-based password manager?

- You can have a different password for each site and it will automatically enter it in your web browser when you go to the login page
- You can generate passwords of long lengths (10, 20, 30 characters) using any combination of characters
- It will synchronize your passwords to all your devices, so if you store the password on your laptop, it will be available immediately on your phone, desktop, tablet, etc. They have browser plugins that assist with these features.
- They can store secure notes and automatically fill out forms with your name, address, and credit card and keep this information encrypted in the application vault

Using LastPass as an example -- although many others offer similar features -- there is also a security challenge which will analyze all of your passwords. This will generate a report that tells you critical information such as: which passwords are being used on multiple sites; which passwords are considered weak and should be changed; which are old and should be updated. It can also automatically update these passwords in many cases. It just makes the whole "password thing" disappear.

There may be a small learning curve when you first start using a password manager, but once you have it down, it will actually be better than not having one even if you only had 2 or 3 passwords -- and it is infinitely more secure.

The main benefit of using these applications -- if it hasn't been hit home enough -- is to prevent reuse of your passwords. Why is that so important? If your password does get compromised in a breach (which is only a matter of time) then the only access will be to the site that was compromised. The first thing hackers do once they crack a password for a login or email address is to attempt to login to the top 50 popular sites with those same credentials and try to gain as much access as possible. So if they get the password to say your old MySpace page (don't laugh it happens all the time) they then will use the same combination against Twitter, Facebook, SnapChat, YouTube,

LinkedIn, GMail, Yahoo!, popular banking and credit card sites, and probably PornHub (it is one of the Top 25 sites on the web), so keep that in mind.

Do you want to know if your email address has been compromised on one of the many breaches? Go to https://haveibeenpwned.com/ and enter your email and I will put $20 right now that you will find your email address has been caught in a data breach (please note that I was referencing Monopoly money, and I still won't pay you). For example, if you have an Adobe account or a LinkedIn account -- you're in there. Then click on the Password menu and enter your "favorite" password that you used to use (you're not doing it anymore, right?) and see if that was de-hashed in one of these breaches. If so, you should immediately go to every account that uses that password and change it, no kidding.

Two Factor Authentication (2FA)

Two-factor authentication (or 2FA) is a second layer of protection in gaining access to your accounts. This is generally something you know (a PIN, High School Mascot, favorite movie, etc.), something you have (e.g. hardware token) or something you are (e.g. fingerprint or other biometric).

Right now I can hear you complaining that memorizing a password is bad enough, now you want me to do even more work to get into my accounts? I can hear you because I hijacked your IoT device and you are not memorizing passwords anymore anyway since you have a password manager, right?

Seriously, you should enable 2FA on any site that supports it. Minimally, you should set up 2FA on any account that you would use if you get locked out of another account or device. This would include your Apple ID account, main email account(s), and definitely any financial site. There are thousands of sites that now support 2FA in some form or another. I will discuss the different types and which are preferred, but any is better than none.

If you want to see an updated list of sites that support 2FA, just visit: https://twofactorauth.org/

Here are some more suggestions on the type of sites where this should be enabled:

Backup and Sync sites
Banking and Payments
Cloud Computing
Cryptocurrencies
Health or Medical related
Tax or Government related (e.g. Social Security)

The main reason to use 2FA is that if your password does get compromised in a breach or someone just happens to know or guess your password, they still cannot get into your account unless they can get past the second level of security.

Although 2FA will take a little extra time to login, it is well worth the effort to set it up and use it. This will save you a lot of grief in the future.

So what are the ways sites implement 2FA? There are generally 4 ways this is generally done, and they are listed here from most desirable to least.

Hardware Token

There are inexpensive hardware devices that plug-into your PCs USB port or connect to your cell phone via NFC that will send a unique key code when prompted. The most popular of these is the Yubikey. The idea here is that you buy several and register them with your critical sites and when you access the site you insert the fob and press the button and it logs you in. I use this method for Gmail, Dropbox, Facebook, and other sites. Someone would have to physically remove this device from you (and know your password) in order to get into your account.

Software Token

Software tokens are implemented typically as mobile phone apps. These authentication applications are nearly as secure and obviously much more common. The two popular ones here are Google Authenticator and Authy. Both are free to download to your phone. You register the app to your site and every time you want to login you just enter the number shown in the app as your secondary login credential. This code is unique to your phone. You can store dozens of site codes in either of these apps. Setting them and registering with sites is relatively painless, typically it means scanning a QR code. If you use this method of 2FA for your site, I recommend it for its simplicity and security.

SMS

This is probably the most common method that online providers use for 2FA. It is definitely better than nothing, but has come under fire recently, and is less desirable than the above two methods. There is a type of hack called "SIM jacking" that is becoming more common. This is where someone calls your wireless carrier and cons the support staff into registering your phone number onto another SIM card. This is easier to do than you think. If that happens, they now own access to all your accounts even if they do not know any passwords. They can just do a password reset and receive the text confirmation message.

I still think this is worth enabling versus having only a password to protect your account. However, I highly recommend visiting or calling your wireless carrier and setting up a PIN that will not allow anyone to make changes (including you) without knowing this PIN. Do not use your birthday or other obvious number for this PIN. This may seem overcautious, and I would have agreed a year ago, but today it is not. Just do an online search on 'sim jacking' and see what shows up.

Here is some help in getting a PIN setup:

Second-level questions

This is the older method of doing 2FA, and not much better than a password, since it is essentially just a second password, but many sites still use it. Unfortunately, it is quite popular with financial institutions who should really be using one of the above methods. Second level questions typically require you to answer 3 questions that you setup previously. Example are: "What was the make of your first car", "What is your oldest niece's first name", or "What was you high school mascot?" The problem with these is that this information could, in theory, be guessed or found using social media.

After all, while there are hundreds of car makers, there are probably 10 that make up the top 90 percent and can be guessed. Is your high school listed on your Facebook profile? There goes that security question to anyone who knows how to Google search. While this is still better than nothing, it is not much better. My suggestion is to always have known answers to these questions that are not true, but that you will not forget. If your school mascot was a Viking, always enter 'chupacabra'. If your mother's middle name is Mary, always use Matilda. This way at least the answers cannot be easily guessed or found via other online searches.

What if I lose my phone or hardware token?

I already know what most of you were thinking; all of the above methods, except the last, are prone to me losing either my phone or hardware token. What do I do then?

This is a valid concern. However, when you setup your 2FA on a given site, you should setup more than one way into the account. Here is an example for a Gmail account.

This account can use a hardware token, or use the Authenticator app, or receive an SMS message. So let's assume this person lost their phone and keys and cannot use any of these methods. Google, in this case, will also generate a series of ten backup codes when you set up 2FA. You can print these out and store them in a safe place. Worst case, you can enter one of these one-time codes to get back into your account.

Every site has a link for 'I've Lost My Device' or something similar which will assist you in getting back into your account or setting up a new device. Be aware, for obvious security reasons, there will be a lot of hoops to jump through. That is why you need multiple ways to get into your account, even if you generally just use one.

Try another way to sign in

Use your Security Key

Get a verification code from the **Google Authenticator** app

Get a verification code at (•••) •••-••32
Standard rates apply

Enter one of your 8-digit backup codes

Get help
For security reasons, this may take 3-5 business days

I know this two-factor stuff sounds like a lot of work, and you may feel it is unnecessary, however, more and more sites will start to require it. Eventually if you don't use it, you will be one of the easy targets. Again, review the previous section on the number of accounts and passwords that have been compromised and understand how easy it would be to seriously impact your life if an important account was hijacked by the wrong person. Like Nike says, "Just do it!"

How do I enable 2FA?

Some site that offer 2FA call it by a different name. It is always best to just check the Help Pages for that site. Below are some high-level instructions for enabling two-factor authentication on the more popular online sites. Keep in mind that this data could be obsolete when you read this, so just search online.

The best way is to use the above mentioned URL (https://twofactorauth.org/) and when you find the site you're interested in, click on the Docs icon next to it and it will take you to the site-specific How-To page.

Chapter 3. Secure Your Web Browser

Arguably, your web browser is the most used application on your PC. It is the main way you access the internet. In fact, I will bet that you spend more than 90% of your computer time on the web browser...unless you are a gamer, in which case, you should get up and exercise a little.

Your browser is the window to the online world, and it is also the window that lets other things into your computer, some of which you may not want. It is also the way third-parties can learn about who you are, what you do, and guess at what you might want in the future. In fact, large online companies now collect so much data on you, that they know you better than you know yourself.

What data that can be retrieved from your browser?

A short list of what data website owners can get from your browser without you even entering anything includes:

IP Address and therefore, your location
Hardware and Software and other technical data
Your browsing history (where have you been on the web recently?)
Which social media or cloud sites you are currently logged into
Your mouse movements
Language
Image metadata for any image uploaded

Here is a sample site that will show you what data can be seen with just a click of your browser: http://webkay.robinlinus.com/

Of course, once you actually start interacting with the website, even more information is gathered. Most of the time this information is just used to enhance your experience at the site (since you bought that, you may enjoy this). However if this data is resold, or stolen, or used in ways unintended later on, you may be giving away important information that might make you vulnerable to security issues either online or off.

The most common way that online sites track your preferences and identify you is via cookies. These cookies store information that will uniquely identify you. Again, most of the time this is not an issue, but now that Net Neutrality has been repealed (in the USA) almost all internet service providers now make lots of money by selling your browsing history, and letting advertisers know where you've been and what you're interested in.

Just for fun, take a peek at everything Google knows about you: https://takeout.google.com/settings/takeout It is actually interesting, eye-opening, and quite intimidating. If nothing else it will make you think twice.

While all websites are required to have privacy policies if you have ever actually read one of these, I think you need some hobbies. They are incredibly boring and obtuse. In addition, they can be changed at the drop of a hat and then your data is now available for whatever they want. Let's be honest, even if you don't mind someone you never met knowing almost everything about you, who likes all those ads following you around on the web?

If you would like to get an idea of exactly what information is collected (and typically re-sold) every time you click a link or visit a site, check out https://whotracks.me/. According to this site:

Google trackers are present on 80% of the web. More than 1/3 of the top websites have over 10 trackers per page.

27% of the web has a hidden Facebook tracking pixel; Facebook knows more than what you just do on Facebook.

So with all of this in mind, are some browsers better than others when it comes to protecting your data? The answer is Yes. So which browsers should be avoided? The two most popular are the biggest culprits for selling you out to the mothership: Internet Explorer; and Chrome. If possible, use an alternative (see below). Chrome, in particular is constantly sending your location and sites you visit to Google, even if you don't use the Google search engine. If you are an Apple person, Safari is generally better at not exposing your data than these browsers.

However, if you do want to stick with Chrome (it's very convenient to use) or IE (seriously?) there are things you can do to minimize the leaky data problem. But first, let's take a look at two great alternatives. Don't worry, modern browsers have made it simple to transfer your bookmarks and preferences in order to reduce switching hassles.

Firefox: A staple in the alternative browser offerings with a die-hard following, it has been around for quite a few years. Mozilla makes this browser available on Windows, MacOS, and Linux. It allows for a lot of user "tweaking" to customize how it can be used and there are many third-party plugins to extend its functionality.

<u>Brave</u>: A relatively new browser that runs on Windows, MacOS, and Linux, as well as Android and iPhone. "Brave blocks ads and trackers that slow you down and invade your privacy." Even though it is based on Google's Chromium code base, it has lots of built-in features to keep your data secure and best of all, it requires almost no setup on your part. It has most of the same conveniences as Chrome and will feel familiar to you if that is your default browser.

For the love of God - Disable Adobe Flash

Flash and Shockwave were once used to provide animation and other interactive aspects to many websites. The downside is that there were many security exploits with it due to the nature in the way it worked, and Adobe had a difficult time keeping up. It is now officially "dead", but some sites still incorporate it into their content. My advice is to avoid these sites until they catch up to modern web design with HTML-5 and other ways to provide the same or better experience. All browsers let you disable Flash in their settings.

Brave it is off by default, leave it off.
Firefox requires a plugin to view Flash; do not load it.
Chrome go to chrome://plugins and click 'Disable' under Flash
IE: I don't know because I'm afraid to start it up, but disable Flash

The Cookie Monster

Cookies are generally needed for a "normal" online experience. Disabling all cookies will generally cause poor functionality or even break the site in your browser. For example, you cannot login to Gmail or Facebook if cookies are disabled. So how can we achieve some balance between "normal" and "broken"? You can eliminate third-party cookies, that is, tracking cookies that are not related to the site you are currently browsing. Third-party cookies offer no direct benefit to users and can potentially be a threat. However most major browser default to allow sites to leave any cookies they want on your machine. This is because the advertisers are their customers; that's why the browser is free.

Here is how to disable 3rd party cookies (3PC) in most browsers:

Brave: disabled by default
Firefox: go to Tools > Options > Privacy;
  uncheck "Accept third-party cookies" and
  click OK.
Chrome: click the wrench icon in the top-right,
  choose Options, Under the Hood, click
  "Content settings", check "Ignore exceptions
  and block third-party cookies from being set."
IE: (sigh) Tools > Internet Options > Privacy >
  Advanced, select Block under Third-party
  Cookies and click OK twice.

Using private tabs - what it is and when to use

Chrome calls it Incognito, and Firefox calls it Private Browsing, and Safari also has it, but what is it actually keeping private? While the details vary between browsers, essentially anything in a private tab or window will not be "memorized" by your browser -- URLs typed; cookies; temporary files. All the data you enter online is still sent over the internet. So are bookmarks and downloads. If you think private browsing will keep your online activities at the office on the down-low, you're probably wrong. In other words, private browsing is not very private. For all intents and purposes, it's still very possible to see what you've been doing.

So why bother with private tabs?
The two best use cases I can think of are the following:

> To login to multiple accounts with different logins. If you have 2 Gmail accounts, for example (one personal, one for your business), you can use a private/incognito tab to login in to them and the credentials from the standard tab will not be used.

> If you <u>must</u> login to an account on a computer that is not yours (e.g. hotel, friend's house) using a private tab will ensure that your login details and URL history will not be available after you close the tab.

If private browsing is not enough to prevent our personal data from being collected and (ab)used by third parties, what can we do instead?

Mandatory Plugins

Regardless of which browser you decide to use there are several plugins/extensions available that can help keep your personally identifiable information from going astray.

HTTPS Everywhere

The Electronic Frontier Foundation (EFF) developed this extension and in their words:
"HTTPS Everywhere is a Firefox, Chrome, and Opera extension that encrypts your communications with many major websites, making your browsing more secure." While unencrypted sites are becoming less common these days, this extension is still too important not to have and requires no effort on your part once installed. This is especially important if you work a lot on public Wi-Fi or away from home. Brave browser has HTTPS Everywhere built into it and can be found in the settings panel.

Privacy Badger

The EFF also created this handy tool as well. Again, after installation very little effort is required on your part for Privacy Badger to do its thing. It automatically learns to block invisible trackers. This one is available for Opera and Firefox only.

Ad Blocker

There are numerous Ad blockers for every browser, however, some take up a lot of computing resources, don't work that well, or have even been found to track you in place of the Ads! So which should you use? Here are the best Ad blockers that will protect your privacy, clean up your browser screen, require little input from you, and not put a burden on your PC.

Firefox: uBlock Origin is the leader here

Chrome: Ad Block Plus is efficient and speeds up the browsing experience.

Brave: There is a built-in Ad Blocker in the Settings panel that is already enabled by default.

Password Manager

Whether you use BitWarden, LastPass, 1Password, or Dashlane, there is an extension that can be added to your browser so that you have a seamless password generation and auto-fill experience. As of this writing, LastPass is the only one that can be installed on Brave - but that might change soon so check the websites. Also, please remember that once this extension is enabled in your browser, turn off the built-in password management feature in Chrome and

Firefox. You do not want to store your passwords in the browser on your local PC!

Canvas Fingerprint Blocking

Fingerprinting is an increasingly common yet rarely discussed technique of identifying individual Web users. We learned in a previous section how much data your browser actually gives up. This technique leverages all of the information that comes from your browser -- fonts, screen size, operating system, plugins, etc. -- and creates a unique fingerprint for you. This way, even if you delete the cookies of the site, they still know who you are. This is a difficult technique to block. There are, however, several plugins that attempt to thwart fingerprinting by adding "noise" to the information such that the website is not sure if it is you or not. Currently, only a small percentage of sites use this method, but it will become more and more popular with ad blocking and cookie cleaning becoming more prevalent. Brave has fingerprint blocking built-in. You can get extensions for Firefox, or Chrome by clicking these links or by searching in the respective extension libraries.

Script Blocking

I do not recommend using script blocking applications for the average user. They tend to require a lot of setup and configuration, otherwise they will "break" a lot of websites that you visit. If you are more technically inclined and want more control over which sites can see your data, you can install NoScript. I also do not recommend turning this on in

Brave browser -- which has a built in feature that is OFF by default. However, if you are technically inclined it will provide more privacy if enabled.

Containers

If you use Firefox, go to the settings menu and click on 'Add-ons' and install Firefox Multi-Account Containers. This add-on helps you keep your online life contained in different tabs. Custom labels and color-coded tabs help keep different activities — like online shopping, travel planning, or checking work email — separate. You can make as many containers as you need.

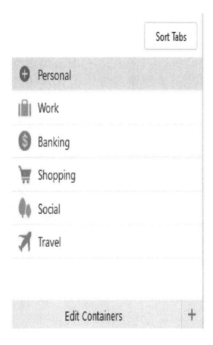

The idea behind this add-on is that cookies and trackers that get created while you browse are not available to other tabs. Normally, if you have Facebook open in one tab, and Amazon in another, and you purchase something from Amazon, Facebook can see this information and uses it to show you ads related to your purchase. Using containers prevents this cross-tab leakage of data.

Browser Tweaks

The following are the recommended settings that offer a good trade-off between security and user experience.

BRAVE: If you are using Brave, then here are the recommended settings. You just need to add your password manager and you're done! The rest of the defaults are good as-is after installation.

CHROME:

Enter "chrome://settings/" in the Chrome address bar and press enter.

Turn off the predictive browser settings since these features send data to Google every time you enter a letter into the navigation bar.

In 'Privacy & Security' disable all of the following features:

> Use a prediction service to help complete searches and URLs typed in the address bar or the app launcher search box
> Use a prediction service to load pages more quickly
> Use a web service to help resolve navigation errors
> Help improve Safe Browsing
> Automatically send diagnostic and usage data to Google
> Use a web service to help resolve spelling errors

Also in this section you should enable 'Safe Browsing' and choose 'Do Not Track'. The latter setting will tell sites you wish to not be tracked, many larger sites will honor this request, but others do not, and they are not under any obligation to do so. Still, it doesn't hurt to turn it on.

When you choose to sync your data such as bookmarks, passwords, browsing history, etc. with Google all of that data will be stored in the cloud. While this can be convenient it does make all of this information available for scraping and used for advertising. You have three choices here: (1) disable syncing altogether; (2) disable some syncing and keep others; (3) keep syncing on and use encryption.

To disable; Go to 'People > Sync' and untoggle 'Sync Everything'.

To disable some data syncing: Go to 'People > Sync' and untoggle various categories. Maybe you want to keep Apps and Extensions. I recommend that bookmarks, passwords, and history not be synced.

If you want to sync all but keep your data protected, Chrome now offers a method to 'Encrypt Synced Data with your own passphrase' listed under the sync options. You will need to enter a passphrase; I suggest using your password manager to create and store it. Either way, be careful not to forget your passphrase. If you forget it, you will lose your synced data.

Next, disable location tracking in Chrome by going to Privacy and security > Content settings > Location and choose 'Blocked'.

Chrome will ask to store email and physical addresses that you type in unless you turn this off. You can use LastPass or other password managers to store this information and provide it securely if needed, so there is no need for this in Chrome.

Go to 'People > Addresses and more' and then
'People > Payment methods' and delete any
information already there and disable these features.

As far as cookies go, below are the recommended
settings for the best privacy and security but the
second step is optional.

Go to 'Privacy and security > Content settings >
Cookies' and enable "Block third-party cookies".
Leave the "Allow Sites to Save & Read Cookies"
enabled! Optionally, if you want to prevent tracking
or if you share a browser with others you can also
enable "Keep local data only until you quit your
browser", but this means you will have to sign into
sites again the next time you open Chrome.

Finally, you should change the default search engine
to either DuckDuckGo or StartPage (see Chapter 4).
Go to 'Search and Assistant' and select from the drop
down list at "Search engine used in the address bar".
Note: Just as this book was published Google
announced that Chrome will now default to use
DuckDuckGo.

FIREFOX:

Go the settings panel, do the following. Under the
"Privacy" tab, complete the following steps:

Select "Use custom settings for history."
Deselect "Remember my browsing and download

history."
Deselect "Remember search and form history."
Deselect "Accept third-party cookies."
Set cookie storage to "Keep until I close Firefox."
Select "Clear history when Firefox closes."

Under the "Security" tab, choose the following settings:

Verify that "Warn me when sites try to install add-ons," "Block reported attack sites," and "Block reported web forgeries" are all selected.
Deselect "Remember passwords for sites."
Verify that "Block pop-up windows" is selected under the "Content" tab.
Verify that "Automatically install updates" is selected in the "Update" tab under "Advanced."
Verify that "Use SSL 3.0" and "Use TLS 1.0" are selected in the "Encryption" tab under "Advanced."

After that is done, enter "about:config" in the Firefox address bar and press enter. Press the button "I'll be careful, I promise!"

Change the following as shown below:

privacy.firstparty.isolate = true
privacy.resistFingerprinting = true
browser.cache.offline.enable = false
browser.send_pings = false
geo.enabled = false
network.cookie.cookieBehavior = 1
webgl.disabled = true
network.IDN_show_punycode = true

To Tor, or not to Tor?

Tor (aka The Onion Router) is a free downloadable browser that uses an alternative set of servers that encrypt and distribute your browsing data so that it is extremely difficult to determine your identity.

This is useful for anyone who wants to keep their internet activities out of the hands of advertisers, ISPs, and Government entities. That includes journalists or activists who live under dictatorships with harsh penalties, people getting around censorship restrictions, law enforcement looking to hide their IP address, or anyone else who doesn't want their browsing habits linked to them.

If you're an average user looking at cat GIFs, watching box opening videos, and browsing Facebook you probably don't need to worry about the government spying on your activity, and Tor is just going to slow down your connection. You need to be secure, not anonymous. There is also no such thing as 100% anonymity, even with Tor. So just skip it and stick to using a VPN (more on that later) and the browser plugins mentioned here.

Chapter 4. Using the Right Search Engine

I think everyone is well aware at this point that Google keeps track of everything that anyone types into the search bar (even if you don't hit Enter) and who is typing it. When you start typing anything in the search bar (e.g. why does my stomach) the auto-complete fills out the most popular next words. There is only one way it can know his - by storing all that data. Typically, this wouldn't be an issue since you probably don't care if Google knows what you typed last week or the month before that. However, there are certain times that you should probably not enter directly into Google. Once you have been profiled or associated with a certain topic be searching for it, it can be hard to divest yourself of it. (But I was just searching for a "friend" - right.)

Here are some scenarios in which you probably want to keep Google and the myriad of advertisers that they sell data to, away from your information.

> Searching for a physical or mental health-related topic: this data could be resold to insurance providers, drug companies. While HIPPA protects actual medical information from being divulged (in the USA), technically it's a gray area stating that you searched for a specific topic. Examples,
>> Diabetes
>> Suicide
>> Multiple Sclerosis

Alcoholism

Medical Marijuana

Abortion

Cialis

Herpes

HIV

Gun and weapons-related information

Financial topics, unless you want every broker and banker to plague you with ads and email. It also sets you up for phishing attacks, since "bad actors" can purchase this metadata as well.

Bankruptcy

Retirement

Taxes

Legal Topics

Divorce

DUI/DWI

Criminal attorney

Anything that has to do with your kids, don't take chances here

Of course, any time you search for something that can be taken the wrong way, even if it is for "fun" (or maybe it isn't in your case) make sure you do not use Google: "how to get back at my neighbors", "the best way to get high with household products", "how to make a Molotov cocktail", well, you get the idea...

I'm sure you can think of other situations that apply to you or your family. Essentially, anytime you are searching for something you wouldn't tell your neighbors or co-workers, you probably want to use a private search engine.

That being said, giving less data to marketers and data resellers is rarely a bad thing. The good news is it is pretty simple to use an alternative search engine and still get Google-like results.
The two websites to use are: DuckDuckGo.com and StartPage.com

DuckDuckGo is based in the USA, and StartPage is a Dutch company.
DuckDuckGo states: "Our privacy policy is simple: we don't collect or share any of your personal information."
StartPage has lots of *about* information on their webpage, but essentially state "The world's most private search engine...it's our belief that personal data should be your data, not Big Data. Period."

Both use Google to retrieve results but remove trackers and personalization and just give you the raw results. So instead of getting what Google thinks you what to see (based on your previous history) these sites give you the actual top results for your search.

The nice thing is that both of these sites make it easy to change your default search engine to their service. DuckDuckGo even has a Chrome extension. I recommend selecting either of these two and change your default search engine within your main browser. It takes 5 minutes (if you're slow) and it will greatly shield your personal information from being sucked into big data.

Chapter 5. Using the Right Email Application

Your Data is My Data

There are two types of email: cloud-based, like Gmail, Yahoo, and Live.com; and Desktop email clients such as Outlook, and Thunderbird. There is an obvious advantage to cloud-based email in that you can access it from anywhere, but there are some downsides that you should at least be aware of if you plan on using it.

Here are some headlines from 2018:
Google admits it still lets HUNDREDS of companies read your Gmail

Google says it's not reading your Gmail, except when it does...

-

It's okay to have a Gmail account, but you might not want to use it for anything serious. I use it to send all my newsletters and sign-up stuff and websites that I know will hammer me with junk later. Not to pick on Gmail, there are numerous articles on all of the big online companies harvesting information and metadata from their users. I believe that you should use an email provider that doesn't read your email or gather data about your conversations to target you with ads.

-

That being said, there are definitely benefits to using Gmail:

  Access from anywhere in the cloud
  Fast searching of your email
  Very good spam identification algorithm
  Built-in antivirus and malware detection
  You can combine multiple accounts
  Built-in calendar/chat/task tools
  Reasonably large amount of free storage

-

So if the good outweighs the bad and you prefer to use Gmail (or Live or Yahoo!), please go ahead, just be aware of the following actions to keep your account safe:

Beware of add-ons and plugins; these third party apps are not Google or Microsoft products. You don't know who they are or what they are doing with your information (see the above article) but by adding it to your webmail as an add-on you are providing full access to your account. Keep the add-ons to a minimum and use ones that have been around a long time and seem well trusted by the community. Don't be a pioneer here!

Under General Settings (Gmail): Choose **Ask before displaying external images** since images pose a risk as infection vectors for malware.

-

If you are considering looking for either a new cloud-based email provider or just seeking an additional account -- maybe for business, or just your close family and friends -- there are some really great alternatives now. All of these services below (unless otherwise stated) have a free tier which is often good enough for personal use, and they have a paid version. These companies make their money from subscription payments and not from reselling aggregated data or by putting annoying ads in your face. They also happen to be quite functional. All of them are privacy and security focused. Looking at the alternatives below you will see that almost all are in countries with strong privacy and data protection laws, i.e. not USA and Canada. Don't let that deter you from giving them a try.

Great Cloud Email Alternatives

Protonmail

Protonmail is based out of Switzerland and is my new favorite email provider. Switzerland has some of the strongest privacy protection in the world. The company founders appear to be American physicists (from Stanford, CalTech, MIT, etc.) who met at CERN. Today they claim to be "the world's largest secure email provider with over one million users."

Protonmail uses end-to-end encryption that is transparent to the end user. ProtonMail uses zero access architecture which means that your data is encrypted in a way that makes it inaccessible even to them. Therefore, no tracking or logging of personally identifiable information can be done. They even make a point to state: "Our primary datacenter is located under 1000 meters of granite rock in a heavily guarded bunker which can survive a nuclear attack." I don't know how much that really matters, and if there is a nuclear attack I'm pretty sure reading my email will not be on the top of my list -- but hey, it's nice that they made use of the basement.

Protonmail has a nice clean, modern interface. Aside from web access there are apps for iOS and Android. The free version allows one email account and comes with only 500MB of storage, but that should be enough if you just use this for critical emails such as your financial transactions and medical information. I subscribe t(and recommend) the Plus version -- it's only about $50 per year and you get 5GB and a ton of extra features including the ability to send encrypted emails to non-Protonmail users. They also have an email client bridge that lets you sync Outlook or Thunderbird to your cloud account if you want to keep your email local.

Another nice feature is that you can send encrypted email to users who do not have Protonmail. After all, your data is vulnerable on your friends email too. When you create a new email to someone you can add a password and expiration date, and also a password hint. The email arrives in the recipient's inbox and it just says they have a message from you with a link and the password hint. When they click the ink it takes them to the message stored on Protonmail server. After entering the correct password they can read it and reply back.

Tutanota

Tutanota is based in Germany and also has end-to-end encryption and 2FA. Tutanota is open source and therefore its code can be scrutinized by experts for flaws. There are apps for iOS and Android and if you upgrade from the free account there is also a desktop application. The free account comes with 1GB of storage. They also have a business level service that allows for central administration of email accounts.

Mailfence

Mailfence is a Belgian-based encrypted email provider. They espouse no tracking, no ads, no third party access to your data, and no one can read your email except you. The free account gets you end-to-end encryption with 2FA and 500MB of storage. The next level of service is only about $3 per month. Mailfence also has contacts, calendar, and notes in a manner similar to MS Outlook.

Disroot

DISROOT.ORG

Disroot is based in the Netherlands and have a grass roots feel to their services. They offer much more than email so take a look at their site. The mail service has a web interface and can sync to your desktop client via IMAP. Unlike the other services they only have a free account and rely on donations for maintaining the software. Your account comes with 1GB of space and a 50MB attachment limit. Disroot uses server-side encryption versus end-to-end, so this is technically less secure than the above solutions but much better than no encryption. You can also use Disroot with Thunderbird and use local encryption to fully protect you information.

FastMail

Fastmail has been around since 1999. They are based in Australia -- which is not generally known for strong privacy laws -- but they have a lot of advantages to their service. First of all there is no free account as this is aimed at business users who want secure email. The interface is very nice and they have most of the advantages of Gmail and Outlook: fast search; good spam detection; calendar; contacts;

mobile apps; and good technical support. All data is encrypted in transport and on the servers and there is an option for 2FA. The cost for a 25GB mailbox is $50 per user per year. If you are a business, Fastmail is definitely worth a look.

Desktop Clients

A ruling by the courts in the USA states:
"Data stored in the cloud for longer than 6 months is considered abandoned and may be accessed by intelligence agencies without a warrant."

This doesn't mean email accounts you haven't logged into in six months, it could be the account you use every day, it just means the messages that were archived for more than 6 months are fair game for all legal and government use.

If this doesn't concern you then continue to use webmail as it is more convenient and the provider performs all backup and software maintenance for you. If you feel that you would rather not store email long-term only in the cloud, then you may want to use a desktop email client. Use an external email client like Thunderbird to download your emails and store them locally. Never leave them on the server.

Desktop email clients can have several advantages to web-based mail:

Access to your email offline; this can come in handy if you get locked out of your account

Store a local copy of your email and back it up in case you ever lose access to your account or the email provider closes down.

Typically desktop clients have a better user interface by tapping into the power of the PC

If you want to change email providers you can just point your desktop client to the new service and you still have all of your old email.

There are a couple of good free desktop email clients including eM Client, and Thunderbird.

Thunderbird has been around for a long time and is widely used. It is made by Mozilla who also created the Firefox browser. If you are familiar with Outlook, you will have no trouble using Thunderbird as an email client, and you will like the price of Free (although please donate if you use it). Thunderbird can connect to multiple email accounts via IMAP/POP so you can consolidate access to all of your web accounts (including Gmail) into one desktop application. There are versions for Windows, Mac, and Linux. Also, there is a free add-on called Enigmail if you want encrypted email.

eM Client runs on Mac and Windows and is visually much more appealing than Thunderbird. It also has email, calendar, contacts, and tasks. It can connect easily to Outlook.com, Gmail, Exchange, and iCloud.

You can connect to 2 email accounts with the free version. If you need more the Pro version is only $49 as a one-time payment.

Protect Yourself from SPAM

So far in this chapter we have talked about protecting you email from prying eyes and gaining access to sensitive information. Another important aspect of staying safe online, as well as just preserving your sanity, is preventing spam and useless messages from clogging your inbox. Spam is also known to carry phishing attacks (see chapter 6), malware, and letters from Nigerian princes. I hear it also clogs your arteries - but that might be a different spam.

There are many times where you need to provide your email address for a one-time transaction and you know you are going to get advertisements and spam until your 80th birthday -- but you cannot proceed without giving out the email address and then possibly even having to confirm by clicking the link in the received email. This is called double opt-in and is generally used due to the CAN-SPAM act. Occasionally there is a site that just wants your email and then gives you direct access to what you wanted. This is typical when downloading white papers and free ebooks. Either way, you do not want to be giving out your good email address for a one time transaction. This might include purchasing tickets to an event, downloading software or information, or posting a reply on a forum. In these cases you should use a burner email address (sometimes called a disposable address). These are also handy for high message count websites such as online forums and newsletters. Another great use for burner emails is for craigslist or other local transaction websites. After selling something online you may want to break contact once the transaction is complete; this can prevent unwanted continued communication.

A burner email will act as a middleman and forward any received emails to the account you specify. Once you no longer need to remain in contact with the website, i.e. the transaction is complete or you are receiving too many emails, you can just delete the burner email address and you will no longer receive any email from that sender.

Some good sites that provide both a free and premium service for mail forwarding burner addresses are BurnerMail and 33mail. Burner will give you 30 free random forwarding addresses and one custom address for free. 33mail will give you unlimited with a 10MB monthly data limit. However, you cannot reply to emails from the 33mail site without a paid account.

My new favorite service in this category is AnonAddy.com. It is very similar to 33Mail, however, it has additional features such as the use of custom domains, PGP encryption keys, and multiple recipients per alias. The paid version is only $1 per month, so if you test it out for free, it probably makes sense to upgrade. The paid version allows up to 50 aliases, more bandwidth, and you can reply from the anonymous email account as well.

Another great alternative is SimpleLogin at https://simplelogin.io/. There is a free plan with 15 aliases to one mailbox and inclues a firefox plugin to generate the alias on the fly. The paid service is $30/year.

Another type of temporary email service allows you to read an email without it ever being sent to your inbox. You can specify an email inbox name --for example, MightyQuinn-- and then view the received email on the web. Note that these are less secure in that anyone can theoretically see the inbox if they type the same name. That's why you should use something uncommon if using these sites. The good news about this type of burner is that you do not have to give out your email address at all, since there is no forwarding.

The 3 best sites in this class of burner email are Mailinator, MailDrop, and GuerillaMail. Each of these has no signup required. GuerillaMail even allows sending of email for free and there is an Android app. These services are best used when you just expect to get a single reply back. For example, when you need to add your email to a web form so that you can download a PDF file or some other information. Do not use them for anything that requires an ongoing communication.

Do not use these services for anything important! If the service becomes unavailable you don't want to miss an important email. Again, these are for online transactions where you are not interested in receiving any further email, or for the forwarding services, you want email but only for a short period of time.

Chapter 6. Go Phish

Phishing attacks are on the rise. Mostly because they work. They say: "A bad day phishing is better than a good day at work". To some cybercriminals, good or bad, phishing is their work.
So what exactly is it? They are emails or online ads that use social engineering and deception to trick you, typically into clicking a link, or responding to an email with sensitive information.

An example might be that you receive an email from Bank of America, of which you are a customer, and the subject says "You're transfer of funds for $5,000 was completed successfully." this of course gets your interest since you didn't transfer any money. The email contains a link "Click here to see the details of this transaction" and this link even says bankofamerica.com in it, so you click it. It takes you to a website that looks exactly like BofA and now you need to login with your username and password. The logins fails. The page refreshes and you login again and this time it works. That's because the first page was a fake and now the bad guys have your login credentials. You breathe a sigh of relief when you see nothing was transferred from your account and figure it was just spam. However, the damage is now done. You should change your password right away!

Many times phishers just send this email to everyone and figure some percentage of people will have an account at this bank. Other times they actually purchase data from online data aggregators on people who are a customer specifically of this bank. Do you still think it's not important to keep your online data travels private?

These phishing attacks include Amazon, Netflix, and any popular site. They increase around Christmas time "Click here for 6 free months of Netflix" "One day only! Samsung 55" TV or $99. Order here.", and they increase around tax time posing as Government emails. Please note that the IRS and most US Government agencies will not randomly contact you via email. If you see an email that says "There was a problem with your tax refund" do not click on any links no matter how realistic the logo or official the text.

As you can see anyone can let their guard down, if you are in a hurry, or it's late at night, or it just so happens you get an email from "Amazon" right after you actually ordered something from Amazon. It's easy to be a victim. These cybercriminals are generally working overseas and due to jurisdictional issues, they are rarely caught or punished.

This type of attack will grow not just because it works but there are now "kits" that anyone can buy on the dark web that automatically emails, tracks, and handles all of the information attack. Another $20 gets you a list of potential victims to email. A couple of sites, Phishtank and OpenPhish, keep crowd-sourced lists of known phishing kits. You can check these out to see what sites are generally targeted (Paypal, Dropbox, UPS, Google Docs, and BofA are prevalent).

Awareness

If you are a person of relatively high-profile, a CEO or CFO of a company of any size, government official, or anyone who might have access to either financial or other information of value, you may be targeted specifically. That is, sometimes criminals will gather information from LinkedIn or Facebook and pose as another employee or one of your friends. They will put information in the email that makes you believe it is them -- only Jim would know that! -- even though you posted it a year ago online and forgot. The email asks you to send some more information about yourself - it might even be something that seems benign like "what was the name of out teacher that we really liked?" which might be a challenge question on your bank account (favorite teacher). Or maybe, they send an email that says "John Smith, CEO has shared a document with you on Google Drive". This link will go to a fake page to try and obtain a login to the corporate drive space; similarly for Microsoft Sharepoint.

Another scam has employees getting emails that looks exactly like it came from the CEO or other executive to transfer money from the bank to the following account. In a big corporation, this works more often than you would think.

Prevention Tips

So how can you protect yourself? Here is a list of tips and techniques that will help you avoid 95% of all attacks. If you do get caught, make sure you change any passwords that might have been compromised and if necessary, alert your bank or credit card company.

> Don't click links in unsolicited emails or on Facebook. If you get an email that seems to come from your bank, instead of clicking the link, just login to your bank account by typing the URL - laziness will end up biting you.

Don't open attachments from unsolicited emails.

Never send passwords or sensitive information via email. If a friend asks for info that you would not want to have compromised, offer to send them a text instead. If the sender balks at this ("I lost my phone!") then you should be very suspicious. Another thing you can do is ask them a question that only they would know and would likely not be on a social media site ("What was your favorite study place in college?" "What was the name of that park we used to play softball?")

Check all email addresses including bcc: before responding to emails.

If anyone ever asks you to move/transfer/send money or ask for financial information in general, validate with the sender via a new email that you compose. "Hey, I got an email asking me to move money to X, just checking - was this you?"

Use two-factor authentication so that even if criminals get your password they still cannot get in.

Inspect any links in an email by hovering your cursor over the link and looking to see what the real URL is - just because it says "ups.com" it may not actually go there. When you hover you might see UP5.com or UPSUSA.com to try and trick you. If the hover link does not match the displayed link, you can be sure it is not a legitimate email. Also, if the site is just an IP address (e.g. http://87.99.34.111/...) <u>never</u> click the link.

If you do click a link from another site or from an email, always check the URL in the browser when you get to the actual site. It should be an https site with a little lock and the URL should be where you thought you were going. This is especially true for smaller web sites that can be compromised.

Use anti-phishing software to detect phishing emails and websites. A free one that works well is <u>Avast</u>.

Chapter 7 Malware, Viruses and Ransomware

You probably have heard of all of these nasty critters. Malware is any malicious software that attempts to invade, damage, take control, or disable computers, networks, or mobile devices. Computer viruses are also a type of malware that also attempts to propagate itself to as many hosts as possible. Ransomware may sound like a cool new movie with Liam Neeson, but even Bryan Mills would have difficulty in getting out of trouble with this new form of sinister attack. Ransomware locks and encrypts all of the data on your PC (and others on the network if you're connected) and you lose access to all of your data. A message pops-up telling you how much money it will cost you to get the decryption key and how to pay. Generally they are looking to get paid in cryptocurrency. Typically there is a time limit (i.e. 48-hours) that if you do not pay all of the data will be erased. Once you realize you have been hit by ransomware, it is probably too late.

Avoiding Malware

According to SecurityWeek "18.5 Million Websites Infected With Malware at Any Time." Remember that even a legitimate site can be compromised and give you a virus. In the past, as an example, big airline websites were targeted and several infected their visitors with malware. That being said, there are certain classes of websites that are more risky than others. Sometimes this is because they are small time sites that lack a corporate security team, and other times it is actually part of their "business plan" to work with malware companies and share the profits.

Websites that are more prone to causing a virus or malware infection:

Sites running WordPress
Pirate and torrent download sites (e.g. free movies, music, software) many hide the malware in the downloaded files
Adult sites

Any site that asks you to download a piece of
    software or codec to view/play files on that
    site

Fake antivirus software (stick to the common top
    10)

Celebrity information sites

Gaming information sites

Online ad links; while Google and Facebook have
    some mechanisms in place to detect links that
    lead to malware, it is not foolproof.

There are several other vectors that can infect your
your PC faster than Typhoid Mary on a kissing spree
for which you should be aware.

Shortened Links: Services like Bit.ly and TinyURL
provide shortcuts for long URLs that are hard to
remember. A lot of sites use these services to also
track effectiveness of marketing campaigns, etc. The
problem is that you do not know where it will take
you until you click it - which can be too late if it leads
to malware. There are several sites which can help
expand the URL before you click on it, one of them
being https://checkshorturl.com/. If it is a bit.ly link
you can get a preview by just adding a plus (+) to the
end of the URL. For example, for
http://bit.ly/Wn2Xdz just enter http://bit.ly/Wn2Xdz+
into your browser and you'll be sent to a preview page
for the link.

Mistyped URLs: One danger that is self-inflicted is
the mistyping of URLs in your browser. We all do it
sometimes. The problem is those who want to cause

havoc also know this and purposefully buy misspelled domains and then setup websites to infect PCs. For example, someone could buy verizom.com (similar to verizon.com) or facebok.com in hope that some people will mistype the URL. Statistics for these mistypes can actually be found online. [By the way, I do not know if the examples here are infected or even real, they are just examples.] The lesson here is to double check your manually entered browser URLs before hitting enter; 'nuff said.

PDF Files: This one is easy to fall victim to since PDF files from Adobe are prevalent and in widespread use. The file needs to be "read" before it can infect your PC. So the best method here --other than not opening a file from an unsolicited source-- is to ensure you have the latest Acrobat reader from Adobe and also do the following:

> Disable JavaScript in the reader
> > Edit -> Preferences
> > Select JavaScript and uncheck "Enable Acrobat JavaScript"
>
> Disable launching of non-PDF file attachments
> > Open the preferences and click "Trust Manager"
> > Uncheck the box "Allow opening of non- PDF file attachments with external applications"

Protecting Against Malware

Even if you follow all of the steps in the previous section, it is still possible that some malware will sneak through and infect your system. It only takes one bad program to cause a lot of damage. If you're "lucky" it just annoys you with constant pop-ups advertising sites and products you have zero interest in ever using. If you are less lucky you might find all of your contacts receiving infected emails (and then all of their contacts) or advertisements. What would that do to your reputation if you run a small business? Of course, another worst case scenario is that the PC becomes unusable and all of your data is missing.

Most good antivirus programs also protect against malware and ransomware, but remember if you are reckless in your computing habits, nothing will save you in the long run. There are some good free options in this category; I recommend searching online but high rankings year after year are generally one of the 3 following programs:

Bitdefender
Avast
Kaspersky

If you have a business you should upgrade and get the Pro version of Bitdefender which is consistently highly ranked, and is not that expensive. It also does not impact overall PC performance very much.

There are some downsides to installing antivirus software. It is important for awareness to list them here, but do not let it scare you away from using it.

Some AV software can adversely affect performance of the PC, especially during scheduled scan times

Some free versions do not automatically update
and this has to be done manually, thereby
making it less effective since you will
probably delay or forget to do this

False Positives do occur; some of your legitimate
software may appear to look like a virus to the
software and can block it from running. Many
programs allow for an exceptions list, but it
can still cause temporary havoc.

Remediating Malware

If the AV software above did not catch the infection -
-possibly because it was too new, or maybe you let it
in by running an attached Word file-- there are other
solutions that can help rid you of the problem.

There are two aspects of remediating ransomware:
remove the infection source; decrypt your files so you
can access them. You may be successful in the first,
but possibly not the second. This is why it is so
critical to avoid them in the first place. Many of the
above AV software tools also contain ransomware
protection, however, this type of attack is changing
every week because it is so lucrative. So keeping up
to date is very important.

In addition to the above AV tools, there are a few
others that can assist in removing malware and
ransomware after being infected. Again, since these

things change from year to year it might be best to do an online search but typically MalwareBytes (PC and Mac) and Trend-Micro have good removal tools for anything your AV software didn't catch.

If you are hit by ransomware you also should look online to find if there are any specific recovery tools for the specific infection you have. The online message you get when your files are locked will generally provide clues to this or state outright the name of the malware. Some example names from the past are: Apocalypse, CrySIS, HiddenTear, Legion, and Xdata. If the ransomware has been around for a little while there is a good chance that you might find a specific antidote that will both remove the infection and recover your files. One place to look for free ransomware decryption tools is on the Avast site at: https://www.avast.com/ransomware-decryption-tools. Another good place to look for help is https://www.nomoreransom.org/en/decryption-tools.html.

If you were hit by ransomware that uses sophisticated encryption (e.g. WannaCry) then the above tools will not help you. If the ransomware was of the locker variety it can shut you out of your computer entirely.

Here are a few more possible methods of removal, although I do not list the step-by-step details here since they are different for Mac, and various versions of Windows, it should be simple to find them online.

Boot your computer in safe mode; run your AV or Malware removal tool from an external disk or USB drive.

Try a system restore in Windows or Time Machine restore for Mac. If you do not have system restore turned on in Windows, you should do it now.

Reinstall your operating system and applications and then download your files from your offline storage or cloud storage.

Your last possible course of action is to pay the ransom to the data kidnappers and hope -- fingers crossed-- that they actually send you the decrypt key. The average payment request according to Sophos is between $500 and $1000. If your data is more valuable to you then that, you can give payment a try but hopefully one of the above fixes worked for you. Better yet, you were able to avoid disaster by following the advice in the book.

Again here are the basic must-do strategies:

Update your operating system and applications

Backup your files offline

Use AV protection and keep it updated

Don't click on links or open documents in email that is unsolicited

Chapter 8 - Securing Your Social Media

Facebook, Twitter, LinkedIn, Instagram, SnapChat, TikTok, and whatever social media site is in fashion this week, are the most visited locations on the internet. Social media can be considered the main gateway of malware. Because most people spend much of their online time on these social networks, hackers put extra effort into taking advantage of these platforms for their own ends.

The big threats on social media are scams, malicious apps, spyware, identity theft, and obtaining private information via social engineering. The malicious apps do not even have to be present on the site itself but in the past have made their way onto social media and into related apps such as TweetDeck or HootSuite, etc. The best way to prevent these threats or at least minimize the damage when something unfortunate occurs, is to limit the information that can be obtained, and to secure your social media applications. These methods are discussed in more detail below.

To Post or Not To Post

Limiting what you post to social media is generally a good idea as oversharing can make you vulnerable to theft, scams, and identity theft. This is also known as operational security. Common sense here should take you a long way, but sometimes things that seem innocent can bite you later. All of this data is there permanently and can be accessed long after you've forgotten about it.

Here are some things you should avoid posting to any social media site to limit your exposure to malicious acts:

Screenshots of personal conversations

Explicit photos of you or someone else

Home address and phone numbers

Your birthday (I know you love those birthday wishes but either change it to something close or hide it, at a minimum do not include the year.)

Banking information - including just the name of your bank

How much money you have, made, or recently came into for whatever reason

False or untrue statements about anyone - it can be considered libel

Confessions - especially if there are legal implications

Your precise location

Anything that might cause you to lose your job ("I hate my boss, what a jerk!")

Your daily schedule or plans for the day/week

Revealing extreme political or religious views

Photos of your vacation - while you are still on it (Hey everyone, my house is empty!)

Pictures of plane tickets or boarding passes

Passport other ID

Shopping receipts

Tagged pictures of kids, yours or someone else's

What you're eating (I just listed this because I want it to stop!)

Also, keep personal and business sites completely separate. Don't discuss work-related issues on Facebook (unless you work there!), and do not put personal views, photos, and opinions on LinkedIn.

Are you my friend?

Prevent being scammed by only accepting friend requests from someone you know. I realize that sounds simplistic but most scams start by accepting friend requests from someone you think you might know, but is not really them. These fake friend requests proliferate for many reasons:

Scammers create fake profiles and request to be your friend to gain access to personal information that you restrict to "friends only."

You may receive friend requests from attackers who post malicious links to malware or phishing sites that end up in your Facebook news feed after you accept the friend request.

They want to sell you something or they sell "guaranteed followers" to others

It could be someone spying on you pretending they know you through someone else; i.e.

private investigator; an Ex; or someone at work checking to see what kind of lifestyle you have outside the office.

How to identify fake friend requests:

Is this someone you already friended? Occasionally people do change profiles but this is rare. Always check if you are already friends with the person.

If you have no friends in common and don't recognize the person then it is probably fake or a mistake. If you do have friends in common, ask the common friend if they know the person and if they got a recent friend request.

If the friend request is of the opposite sex and quite attractive and you do not know them, it is likely someone phishing for information or to sell something.

Does the person have a recent account? If they just created their account in the last month it is almost certainly fake. Is there content on the site? If you did end up accepting the friend request and you do not see many friends or very few posts, this is suspicious.

If you get a direct message from someone you are already friends with and the message seems "off" or suspicious (e.g. "Scott would never use the word Disingenuous") then their account may have been hacked. A good way to test this is to ask (via DM) about something personal that only that person would know and would NOT have been posted on their social media. In other words, a pets name is not a good question. "Hey man, I was just thinking about that time in 6th grade that we all got in trouble for that food fight. What was that teacher's name again?" If they don't know and you think they should, that could be a warning. Also, maybe you made up the whole event, so if they answer "I can't remember either" you know it is not them.

If anyone ever asks you for money online it is almost definitely a scam. If you think it is really that person, have them call you and hopefully you would recognize their voice. If not, you're not close enough to lend them money.

For any of these requests where you think you know the person and have access to another contact method, email, phone, another social media profile, always contact them and ask if they tried to request a connection.

Securing your social media

It is not possible to go through the exact steps to secure your account for every popular social media platform, but the more common ones are presented below. For others, find the settings panel and simply go through each setting. Since the user interface for

53

applications changes frequently you can always do an internet search for step-by-step instructions.

Also, keep in mind that it is not likely that you can completely secure your personal data on social media platforms that make their living off of gathering and selling your data. That doesn't mean, however, you have to be complicit. Since the obvious answer for better privacy on social media is to not participate, below is a description of some ways to lower your data footprint for those who are not yet ready to abandon them.

Facebook

Something you should do both before and after making the changes below is to see how you Facebook profile looks to others. You can do this by going to your Facebook page to the right of your name, click 'View As'. This will allow you to see what is public on your profile- i.e. not your 'Friend'. This will allow you to check if you are sharing anything publicly that you don't want to share.

The first and most important step: Limit the data you provide in your profile. In the About section, remove any information that is not important for you to share. This means your current hometown, your high school, current location, life events, etc. You should also remove your birthdate, or better yet put a fake date. If you love those birthday wishes, at least remove the year you were born. All of this can be used to attempt identity theft, or hack into your accounts (what was your high school mascot?) -- all of your friends should already know where you live or where you used to live. Some people even go as far as to change their name. You can use first and middle name or repeat your first name twice. Apparently Facebook requires two names - so tough luck on Madonna and Beyonce.

Your photo is another piece of information that can be used against you. Facial recognition technology has become very sophisticated and your name attached to a photo can be used for all types of purposes you never intended. It might be best to use a photo that is not your face as your profile (or background) pic. Here are some alternatives:

> A picture of your cat (those seem to be popular)
> Make a drawing of your face or use one of those caricature drawings from the carnival
> A picture of an item in your house that cannot be associated with you
> A silhouette photo of yourself
> An abstract photo that you took

You should not use any copyrighted pictures (e.g. Homer Simpson, even if you do look like him), or another live person. You can get a photo of a person that does not exist at https://thispersondoesnotexist.com/ and use that.

About

Overview

Work and Education

Places You've Lived

Contact and Basic Info

Family and Relationships

Details About You

Life Events

Once you have scrubbed your personal details from the About page, the rest of the settings below can be changed from the top-right dropdown menu and then selecting Security, Privacy, and Timeline and Tagging.

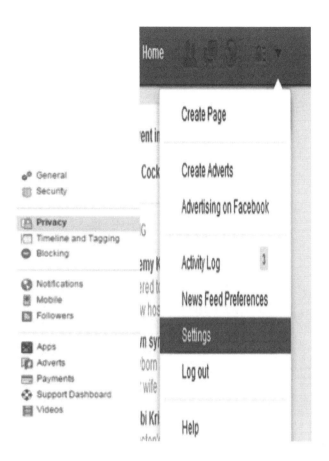

Limit friend requests

To avoid getting friend requests from strangers, right-click the drop down arrow at the top right and select Settings and select Privacy on the right-hand side. Under 'Who can contact me?' select Friends of friends.

Hide your Friend list

Click on your name on the top menu bar. Across the middle of the screen running horizontally you'll see options for Timeline, About, Friends, Photos and More. Click Friends. Next to Find Friends you'll see a pencil - click this and select Edit Privacy. Click the drop-down arrow next to Friend List and select Only Me.

Control Tagging

Click on 'Timeline and Tagging'. Make sure that only 'Friends' can post and see things that others have posted on your Timeline. You will also want to make sure that only Friends can see things that you've been 'tagged' in, i.e., something that somebody else has posted about you. Add an extra layer of security by turning on 'Review

Tagging	Who can see posts you're tagged in on your timeline?	Friends	Edit
	When you're tagged in a post, who do you want to add to the audience of the post if they can't already see it?	Friends	Edit
Review	Review posts you're tagged in before the post appears on your timeline?	On	Edit
	Review tags people add to your posts before the tags appear on Facebook?	On	Edit

Limit who can see posts new and old

Click the drop-down arrow at the top right, select Settings and click Privacy from the options on the right. Look for Who can see your future posts? and click Edit. In the drop-down menu make sure Friends is selected.

Even if your account is private, your old posts may still be public.

Under 'Who can see my stuff?' look for the option Limit the audience for posts you've shared with friends of friends or Public and click the Limit Past Posts link on the right. The menu will expand. Click Limit Old Posts. A warning box will appear. Click Confirm.

Opt-out of advertising tracking

Go to your Facebook ad preferences and choose:

"Ads based on data from partners": not allowed

"Ads based on your activity on Facebook Company Products that you see elsewhere": not allowed

"Ads that include your social actions": not allowed

Remove 3rd Party Apps

Go to the Apps and Websites section of your privacy settings and remove any apps or sites that you're not using or security that you don't trust.

Location History

Settings --> Location History

Turn it off.

A final word about Facebook Messenger: Don't.

This is truer for cell phones than your desktop. Do not load either the Facebook app or messenger on your phone. If you want to access Facebook from your phone use the web browser. While we are not delving into cell phone security in this book, Facebook scrapes data from many other apps on your phone even if you don't use it.

Twitter

Go to Settings → Privacy & Safety from the profile photo menu.

For photo tagging: choose 'Do not allow anyone to tag me' (recommended)
For Tweet Location: unchecked
Let others find me by my email address and phone number: unchecked
Address book: Remove any contacts that have been stored in Twitter.
Tailor Twitter based on my recent website visits: unchecked, and choose Do Not Track.
Tailor ads based on information shared by ad partners: unchecked, and choose Do Not Track.
Receive Direct Messages from anyone: unchecked (keep those scammers at bay!)

Account section:
Require personal information to reset your password: checked
You can turn on login verification which will send

you an SMS code each time you attempt to login. You then enter the code to gain access to your account. This is a weak form of 2FA but if you have a popular Twitter account you should consider enabling it.

Email Notifications section: Disable as much as possible; Twitter is very "noisy" with email.

Your Twitter data section: Go to the apps tab and verify all applications with access to your account. You can also download all of your data from here.

Instagram

You should prevent disclosing your location when posting. If you already have location data in your Photo Map you can clear this out by clicking the location icon in your profile, tap on the pictures you want to remove, select edit, select deselect all, select done, confirm your selection, select done.

Turn off activity status so that other users cannot tell when you're online: Go to the button at the top of your menu and hit Settings. Scroll down to Privacy and Security> Show Activity Status;toggle the option to off.

Enable 2FA from the menu at Privacy and Security> Two-Factor Authentication. Toggle Require Security Code.

Disable Location tracking from the menu at Privacy and Security> Select Location Services. Turn off location access by specific apps, or toggle off location access to all apps entirely.

Other tips:

> Limit the access of third-party apps
> Block users that spam you or ask for money or
>> any other suspicious or annoying activity.
> Consider making your account private

SnapChat

Open Snapchat and tap your profile picture/Bitmoji icon in the top right of the screen. Tap the gear icon in top right to go to your settings:

> Enable 2FA
>> Find Two-Factor Authentication in the settings option. Tap the button beside Authentication App and follow the online instructions to complete.
>> [Also it makes sense to setup the Recovery Code option.]
> Only Let Your Friends Connect
>> Look for the Contact Me option and choose 'My Friends'
> Only Let Your Friends see Stories
>> Look for the View my Stories option and choose 'My Friends'
> Don't let others see your current location
>> Look for the See my location option and choose Custom and don't select anyone.

Prevent your phone number from being used to
    friend you
    Look for Let others find me using my mobile
    number and turn this off

Third Party Apps and Logins

When you agree to allow one application to allow
sign-in from another application you are effectively
granting permission for these applications to share
data. So if you visit a site and are able to login with
your Facebook or Google account, these sites are
connected with your identity. While this is a great
convenience, it also presents a vulnerability in that all
f your data on all of these sites are only as well
protected as the weakest link. If you are using a good
password manager you have less of a reason to allow
third-party app connections. The only reason to allow
this would be if there is a distinct advantage of
combining data from both sites.

So the point is 'be choosy' on which applications you
connect permissions for, and secondly to check these
permissions occasionally. Many times you may
connect a site or application and then stop using it
shortly thereafter, however, the connection still exists
and can provide a backdoor to your data.

Here is how to check which apps are connected to
your Google account:

Login to Google

Click on our photo at the top right, and then click
    on My Account.

Go to Sign-in & Security and select Apps with
    account access.

Click Manage Accounts

Check the lists for apps that are unfamiliar or that
    you no longer use. Click on one of the apps
    you want to remove permissions. Click on
    Remove Access.

To remove access to your information to third-party
apps (like all those games you never play anymore,
we're looking at you Farmville), go to Facebook
General Account Settings page, scroll down and
select Apps and Websites in the left-hand menu. Look
on the Active tab and choose the apps you no longer
need and click 'Remove'. Remember that this does
not delete your account on the connected application,
it just removes the connection between Facebook and
the other site. You can still login directly to that site
with your login, you just can't use your Facebook
login

Old accounts

Do you have an old MySpace account? What about
Tumblr? Many times we sign-up for a new social
application only to lose interest and abandon it
several months (or years) later. The thing is your

account is likely still active unless you purposefully closed it. If someone were to hack into this -- maybe they got the login information because these abandoned sites are easy hacking targets-- they could gather your information and/or impersonate you on that account. Hopefully, at this point you are not using that same password, but if so now all other accounts using it are vulnerable. Best practice here is if you haven't used an account in 6 months and don't see a reason to do so in the near future, close the account. If you aren't able to close it, then change all of your personal data to made up information, and change the password to something really really long.

Chapter 9 - Windows 10 and Microsoft Office Security

While this chapter title might seem like an oxymoron, the truth is that Microsoft has actually spend a lot of time and money on improving security for their most recent O/S and applications. Granted, they have taken a step backwards on user privacy, but compared to past implementations, the security is much better. That being said, there are still some steps you should take if you use these tools either on the PC or in the cloud.

Windows 10 Security Settings

To ensure data security use of encryption is the best bet; this is discussed in Chapter 13.

Create a Local User

Instead of having to login with a Microsoft online account (like live.com, etc.) use a local login just like the good old days.

Settings > Accounts > Your info. Click 'Sign in with a local account instead' and follow the instructions.

Turn off SMB1

SMB1 is an old technology, and recently the WannaCry ransomware took advantage of it on older computers. To disable this feature do this--

Press the Windows key

Start typing Turn Windows features on or off and select the Turn Windows features on or off Control Panel item.

Scroll down and uncheck the box next to SMB 1.0/CIFS File Sharing Support

Press OK (you may have to restart)

Turn on Windows Restore

Type "Create a restore point" in the search box and choose Control Panel.

From the "System Properties" dialog box; Go to "System Protection" tab and choose your Windows installation drive (usually drive C).

Click on the "Configure" button. Choose 'Turn on system protection" and click OK.

Remove Bloatware

Go to Start> Settings> Apps.
Check the installed apps under "Apps & feature" section.
Uninstall anything you will not be using.

Turn on Windows Firewall

Go to "Control Panel > System and Security > Windows Defender Firewall".
Click on the link "Turn Windows Defender Firewall on or off" from the sidebar.
Enable the firewall option for all the listed networks - but definitely for Public!

Windows 10 Privacy Settings

This will be a longer section than the previous because Microsoft is about as private as your 10 year old sister who just found out you did something Dad will hate. Windows 10 has many built-in "features" that supposedly enhance your experience within windows and its supported applications. However, many of these are extensive breaches to personal privacy. Here are the top settings that you may consider changing to protect your data:

Turn Off Location Determination

Settings > Privacy > Location and the Change button under Location for this device is on and toggle it Off.

Syncing information across devices

Settings > Accounts > Sync your settings. You can either turn off all syncing at once, or you can toggle individual settings on/off.

Go Away Cortana

Personally, I would turn off this feature (a personal assistant similar to Siri or Alexa) but if you like the convenience, at least do the following --

Turn off Cortana on the lock screen Settings > Cortana > Talk to Cortana; toggle off 'Use Cortana even when my device is locked'.

Disable Advertising ID

Each Microsoft account has a unique advertising ID that lets the company collect information about you. You will still get ads but you can keep them gloriously less applicable by --

Settings > Privacy > General; toggle off 'Let apps use advertising ID to make ads more interesting to you based on your app usage'.

Turn off Delivery Optimization

This lets your PC share updates with others on the network in the background.

Settings > Update & Security > Windows Update > Advanced Options > Delivery Optimization.

Turn off Shared Experiences
Settings > System; toggle off 'Shared experiences'

Control App Access to Your Account Info and other Data
Settings > Privacy > Account Info; toggle off 'Let apps access my name, picture and account info'. Now go through Settings > Privacy and each of the other left-hand options: Calendar, Contacts, Call History, etc. and decide to either disable it or pick and choose which apps can access this information.

Turn off Feedback and Diagnostic Info
Settings > Privacy > Feedback; change the settings to Basic, Off, Never.
Under App Diagnostics; toggle off.

For more comprehensive privacy on Windows 10, you can download one of the 3 popular free tweak tools online: AntiSpy for Windows, W10 Privacy and O&O Shutup10.

O&O Shutup10 Anti-spy software is the easiest to use in my opinion. You just slide the switch to on or off for the specific security or privacy setting. This software is entirely free and does not have to be installed – you just run it.

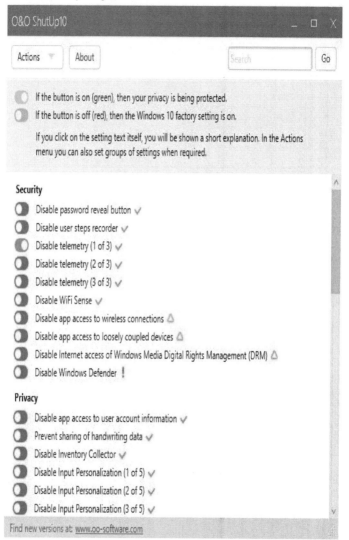

Whichever of these you choose, remember that you will need to re-run it again every time there is a windows update, since Microsoft is in the habit of turning many of these items back on for what they feel is a better perceived "user experience".

Microsoft Office Settings

Believe it or not, recent versions of Microsoft office, both online and in the cloud have very good security settings enabled by default. The main issue here is ensuring that you keep up with the most recent patches. If you have changed some of these settings in the past here is a very quick rundown of the important settings to protect yourself:

Open any application in Microsoft Office (Word, Excel, PowerPoint) and click on the File menu and then Options. In the General window, find the section for Office intelligent services. The option to Enable services should be turned off by default.

At the Options window, click on the button for Trust Center Settings.

Click on the category for ActiveX Settings. The default is to run ActiveX controls in Safe mode. Also choose "Prompt me before enabling all controls".

In category Macros: Choose "Disable all macros with notification".

71

Next, click on the category for Protected View. This option is critical to protect yourself when accessing downloaded or attached documents since it opens the file in read-only mode. The default is to enable it for files from the Internet, files from possibly unsafe locations, and files attached to an Outlook email. Check all the boxes here and make sure this is enabled!

Next, click on the link to File Block Settings. Ensure that the setting here is to open older types of files in Protected View.

That should keep you relatively safe when using Microsoft office. As always, if you get a prompt because a script or macro wants to access your computer -- always read the message and think twice on whether you need to allow this. You can always click No and see if the file provides the information you need.

Side Note: Secure Chat

Just a quick side note for secure chat communication. Chat is still popular with many people, but most chat clients do not protect the data typed into the interface at all and most are evaluating what you type for data and marketing purposes (we're looking at you Facebook). There is a way to communicate with all your chat peeps and still keep the conversation on the downlow. Pidgin is a chat program which lets you log in to accounts on multiple chat networks simultaneously. Pidgin can communicate with AIM, Facebook Chat, IRC, Steam, WhatsApp, TorChat, Skype, and many others, all from one interface. Adding the Off-the-Record Messaging (OTR) plugin can provide secure and private end-to-end chatting even over not secure chat platforms.

Pidgin runs on Windows, Linux, and if you want an equivalent for MacOS try Adium.

Chapter 10 - Secure Note Taking

Storing notes and other important information in an organized fashion is very convenient and can enhance your productivity. While there are many popular note taking applications, the 2 best known are Evernote and Microsoft OneNote. Both of these services have a free version and a paid version with more storage and features. They also have phone apps to help you store and retrieve from your mobile device. The data you store in these services resides both on your local PC (or phone) and in the cloud on the provider's servers. So the question is how safe and secure is your data? Reviewing the data breaches from Chapter 1 should remind you that even though Microsoft and Evernote seem to use encryption and good data policies in place it is likely that there could be a breach as well.

More likely, someone could get access to your account via one of the methods described in the previous chapters.

If you are going to rely on one of these note taking tools, then following the suggestions below should help you and your data stay safer. If you are really concerned about whether Evernote or Microsoft are scanning your data or that are reselling it (there is no evidence for that at the time of this writing) then you can use the suggestion for a more secure solution below.

Cloud Note Security Practices

The advice here is similar to storing data on any cloud service. First and foremost, don't store any data that would be possibly devastating if it were to get into the wrong hands. This includes but is not limited to:

Social security numbers
Picture of your passport or driver license
Medical information
Usernames and passwords
Bank account or credit card account numbers or
    related information
Detailed information about your children
Any information that could compromise your
    safety

Any information that could harm your business

In addition, use the following safe computing techniques that were discussed in the previous chapters:

Use a unique and complex password with adequate length

Don't login using another account, i.e. Google, Facebook, etc.

Do not add third-party extensions/apps since you will be providing full access to your data

To see which applications can access your data in Evernote, go to your Evernote Account, --> Settings / Security / Applications. Revoke access to anything you do not really need.

Use 2FA; this is supported by Evernote from your Account settings. OneNote will support 2FA if you set this up at the Microsoft Account, Security & Privacy settings.

Encrypt text in your notes

Unfortunately Evernote does not let you encrypt a notebook, or even a note for that matter. However, you can highlight any text and right-click and encrypt with a password. I am not sure how strong this encryption is, but it is better than nothing. To decrypt the text, click on the encrypted text and select 'Show encrypted text'; you will be prompted for the password.

OneNote allows you to password protect (via password) an entire section (i.e. tab). Right-click 'Password protect this section'. It will remain unlocked for a period of time and then auto-lock again. You can adjust the amount of time under File → Options.

Warning: If you forget your password, there is no way to retrieve it and cannot unlock your notes. Make sure you use a reliable password manager.

Use a local notebook; Evernote allows you to create a notebook that does not sync to the cloud and is only stored on your PC. Obviously you cannot access this information from other devices.

Standard Notes

In lieu of the big data companies above storing your data and then encrypting it on their servers after the fact, there is another option where you completely control all access to your notes - but still retain the convenience of the cloud features. Standard Notes is available for Windows, MacOS, Linux, iPhone, Android, and via web browser. The software is open source and does not perform any tracking or show any ads. Standard Notes is free to use on all platforms, for unlimited devices, and this includes cross-platform synchronization and no data limits.

Your notes get encrypted on your device, i.e. before they are stored on the cloud, and only you can see them. The connection between your device and the server is always provided via a secure connection. The only limitation is that it is for text only, no images. Even so, it is too good of a deal to pass up. If you protect your account with a strong password you could even store information that is not recommended to store on other cloud services since there is no way for anyone to scan or steal it. Once again, if you do lose your account password, it cannot be recovered and access to your notes is gone. Use a password manager!

If you decide to upgrade to the Extended Plan (it's inexpensive) you can get additional benefits:
    Two-factor authentication
    Encrypted attachments for your notes stored
        directly in your Dropbox or Google Drive.
    Note version history (up to 100 years!)

Additional editors and themes.

Automated encrypted backups of your notes to Email, Dropbox, OneDrive, or Google Drive

I have slowly migrated from Evernote to Standard Notes. I use Evernote for data I want to share with others (via link), or for temporary research or data that requires images but is not too sensitive. Also, any data that would not be disruptive if it found its way into someone else's hard drive (e.g. recipes, poems, book lists, etc.)

Open Source Alternative: Look at Joplin for private notes which includes end-to-end encryption as an option.

Chapter 11 - Deleting Files...for Reals

It is pretty well-known at this point that when you delete a file from a PC, it does not actually delete the data, it just removes the file reference from the list and marks the space available for storing data. If you want to see just how much of your data is recoverable, download the free Recuva tool and check out the list of files from possibly even years ago. Maybe you can use some of those photos as throwback postings (or not).

The point is delete is not really delete. Think of it more as putting it on a shelf and saying I'll get to throwing this out someday. The good news is that there are several good (and free) utilities that can help permanently delete one or all files. Also, newer PCs tend to have a solid state (SSD) disk versus the older magnetic hard disks. Although if you have more than one drive in your PC, there is typically a mix of SSD and HDD. Using a SSD disk does tend to make it harder to retrieve information post-delete, but still not impossible. So should you download one of these apps?

While I believe you should always use permanent delete tools, here are some instances that are considered "must-do":

Selling your PC (quick format is <u>not</u> good
      enough!)
Disposing of your PC
Removing sensitive files (e.g. financial data,
      passwords, official documents and photos)

Two great free applications are <u>Eraser</u> and <u>File Shredder</u>. Eraser's interface also allows you to create scheduled erasing tasks, so you can set up a weekly/daily schedule to wipe anything in your trash bin. Another good option is the previously mentioned <u>Recuva</u> app; it also allows for full deletion.

On SSD-based Mac, right click and select Move to Trash, then open the Trash app and select Delete Permanently or Empty Trash. However, if you want to make sure the deleted files are 100% unrecoverable, you can use CleanMyMac. You can also look on the Mac App Store in iTunes and download a free utility. For magnetic hard drives you must make sure that you clean files even after they are emptied from the trash. These same utilities can be used.

Chapter 12 - Encryption

Encryption will make all of the data on your PC inaccessible to anyone who doesn't have the key (unless they work for the NSA). Many corporations now require that business PCs and phones have encryption enabled by default to prevent lost/stolen devices from spilling sensitive corporate or customer data. If your device is unencrypted, hackers will have access to anything stored on that device, including photos, emails, documents, and contacts. You should enable encryption on every phone and computer you use.

Encryption is totally legal in North America (as of this writing) and in the EU. There is also a bill called the Encrypt Act (2018) which has been submitted to the US House of Representatives that will preempt US States data security vulnerability mandates and decryption requirements. MacOS and MS Windows (Pro versions) both come with built-in encryption. There are also open source solutions to encrypt your PC if you have another operating system (e.g. Linux) or prefer not to use a large corporation encryption method.

Important: Using VPNs (see chapter 16) and/or the use of SSL/HTTPS only encrypts your data "in-flight" not while it is resting on your hard drive or cloud folder. Safeguarding your data on your computing device requires encryption. There is a much greater chance your data will be stolen or accessed while sitting on a storage device than during a transaction. So encryption is really the best defense for preventing unauthorized access and use.

If you tried encryption in the past and had a bad experience, modern encryption will not slow the performance of your PC or applications (although boot up time may be a bit slower). It is also very simple to use, and in fact you really do not need to do anything once you turn it on other than remember your passphrase.

Windows Encryption

Many new PCs that ship with Windows 10 will automatically have "Device Encryption" enabled. The only drawback here is it only actually encrypts your drive if you sign into Windows with a Microsoft account, not a local account. Your recovery key is then uploaded to Microsoft's servers in case you lose it.

To verify: Settings --> System --> About, and check for "Device encryption"

If you happen to have Windows 10 Pro or Enterprise you can use BitLocker instead. Just search for BitLocker in the Start menu and click Turn On Bitlocker. You will need to remember your BitLocker key; you will be able to download a local copy as well.

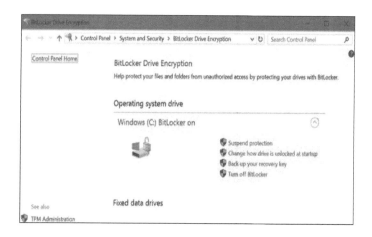

VeraCrypt

If you don't have Windows 10 Pro or do not want to store your key with Microsoft, VeraCrypt will allow you to encrypt your Windows 10 PC's system partition for free. It encrypts a partition or drive where Windows is installed with pre-boot authentication. VeraCrypt is a free open source disk encryption software for Windows, Mac OSX and Linux.

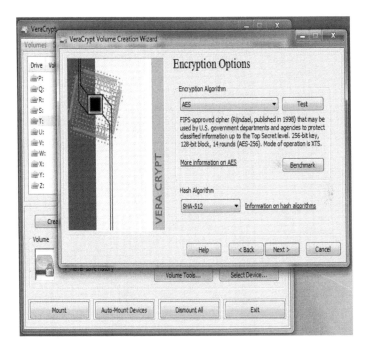

Mac FileVault Encryption

When FileVault is turned on, your Mac will always require that you log in with your account password.

> Choose Apple menu --> System Preferences, then click Security & Privacy.
> Click the FileVault tab. Click Locked, then enter an administrator name and password.
> Click Turn On FileVault.

You have the options to store your password in case you ever forget it:

> Download a local recovery key (you should at least do this one, but obviously don't store it on your Mac!)
> Save to iCloud
> Store with Apple and access via 3 security questions.

Chapter 13 - Cloud Storage Security and File Sharing

Cloud Storage is the defacto way to save your files these days. You're probably already using cloud storage in some form or another. iCloud, Google Drive, Box, Dropbox, Amazon Web Services, etc. Cloud storage has lots of advantages: offsite storage of your files in case of fire; ease of access from anywhere and any device; files can be shared with others easily; and most services provide online collaboration. The cloud will continue to be essential for both personal and business use of file storage.

One problem is that these services work directly with the Government (i.e. NSA and FBI) and their Terms of Service specify that they have the right to look into your files. Since they can look into your files they can search for keywords and sell this information to advertisers. This means if you have a lot of business documents on Google drive (for example), they are potentially being scanned and indexed. Another issue is that cloud accounts can be breached or hacked and competitors can steal your valuable data or your personal data can be offered for sale on the dark web. This is especially important for businesses that have HIPPA or SOX compliance data on their cloud drive. Additionally, having your files encrypted in the cloud will help prevent them from being corrupted in a malware or ransomware attack.

In this chapter we will present some options for keeping the benefits of cloud file storage while maintaining security of your data.

One solution could be to encrypt your files locally and then move them already encrypted to your cloud drives. You could have a folder on your PC encrypted via VeraCrypt or other utility and then sync it to the cloud. The problem with this is that you will need the decryption key on every device that you might access these files. If you only use one computing device then this solution will work, however, it is probably not for most people.

The two other possibilities are to either: (1) use a third-party encryption tool that encrypts/decrypts files between your devices and the cloud storage providers; or (2) use a cloud storage provider that includes encryption in their solution.

Third-Party Encryption Tools

Most likely you are using one or more of the popular cloud storage providers such as Google Drive; Dropbox; Microsoft OneDrive; Apple iCloud; or Box. These are popular because they give away free storage as an entry level feature and are integrated with the vendor's other products. They are also stable companies and are not likely to disappear overnight taking your data with them! If you use one of these services and want to encrypt some or all of the data stored there, there are several third party tools to help you. At a minimum you should consider having at least one folder that contains secure and sensitive information and encrypt it. An example might be your tax return information or copies of your passport. If you are a business, your financial reports and customer lists might go in this folder.

The two encryption solutions that have been available for both Windows and MacOS for some time are BoxCryptor and Cryptomator. Both of these tools provide strong encryption and a transparent interface that allows you to use your files like working with any folder or USB drive.

BoxCryptor can encrypt files between all of the above cloud storage providers, plus Amazon and a lot more. The free version allows you to encrypt only one of the above providers and access files from 2 devices. You can get unlimited providers and devices for less than $50 per year. It works on Windows, Mac, Linux and both iPhone and Android.

Cryptomator is a free open source client-side encryption for your cloud files. It also works on Windows, Mac, Linux and both iPhone and Android. From their website:

> "Transparent encryption means you will not notice any difference in working with your files. While the vault containing your encrypted data resides somewhere in your cloud folder, Cryptomator provides a virtual hard drive through which you can access your files.
> You can work on this drive as if it were a conventional USB flash drive."

I use Cryptomator for all of my cloud storage and create individual folders on each and use a strong password as my vault password. If you are a small business you should consider the BoxCryptor paid plan.

Encrypted Cloud Providers

If you prefer to avoid the third-party tools and you are not adamant about using Google, iCloud, Dropbox or one of the other common cloud storage providers, there are other cloud drive solutions that include end-to-end encryption. All of these providers are zero-knowledge encryption which means only you have the key and no one can access your data, even the provider. Again, make sure you do not lose the recovery key or your password otherwise your data is unavailable.

Mega was owned by Kim DotCom and is established in New Zealand. This is probably the best choice for individuals (versus business). You can get 50GB for free; and 200GB for about $5.50 per month. You can access your data from any web browser or from the desktop app or via your mobile phone. You can also allow sharing and collaboration of your files if needed.

Another established solution is Tresorit. They are focused on businesses -- including small and solo freelancers -- and there is no free option. This is a Swiss-based company; Switzerland is renowned for its policy of neutrality and strong data protection laws. They are also GDPR compliant if that pertains to your business. You can upload and access your files with from any desktop and mobile device using Windows, MacOS, Linux, Android, iOS, and from any browser. They have plans starting around $12 per month for 200GB and enterprise-level pricing up to 1TB. Check the website for details.

SpiderOak is based in the USA and is also focused on business accounts. They offer several products including a file sync backup solution, as well as a secure collaboration software tool. If you need encrypted secure files but also need to share and collaborate a lot between people and groups, this is your best solution. Government agencies use SpiderOak to protect their project files while working across teams.

pCloud is a Swiss company that started out by backing up photos for professional photographers. Now you can back up and share all of your files to the cloud and access them from just about any device. Over 10 million users trust this service with their files. It will backup directly from Facebook, Dropbox, Instagram, OneDrive, as well as your hard disk. If you also download pCloud Drive you can access your files in the cloud as if they were just another drive on your PC, but without taking up any additional space. You can get 10GB for free just by signing up. This is a good way to test out the interface and see if it fits your needs. If you like it, you can get 500GB for $50 per year, or 2TB for $95. They also have lifetime subscriptions available. This is the service I currently use and find it intuitive and fast.

A newer contender in this space, out of the UK, is IceDrive. This is a similar service to pCloud. You can also get a 10GB free account and test it out. You can also get 1TB for $50 or 5TB for $180. So if you need more than the 2TB that pCloud provides, this could be your option. The lifetime subscriptions are also much cheaper than pCloud since I suspect that IceDrive is trying to gain attention in this space. There is no reason why you cannot have free accounts with both services and try them for yourself.

If you are more technically inclined and prefer to completely control your data, you can install NextCloud on a local PC with attached storage and create your own encrypted cloud storage. It also can connect to DropBox and other offsite solutions. There are apps for mobile phones and desktops, but generally you can drag and drop files straight from your browser. This is a free and open source project and all support is via online community. Installation is relatively straight-forward but some configuration will require a bit of technical prowess and persistence.

Sharing a File Securely

If you have a file that contains a lot of personal information and you need to share it with one person, you have several options. If you are using one of the encrypted file services above (e.g. pCloud) they have a mechanism that allows you to share a file with anyone that has an email address. Hopefully, you know not to upload and share this file via Dropbox or Google Drive by now!

If you do not want to use an encrypted cloud service or just want to quickly share a file on your hard disk, there are a couple of online sites that provide the ability to store a highly encrypted file online for a specified period. Let's assume the scenario is you have a zip file of all of your tax documents that you need to pass to your accountant. Password protecting the ZIP file and sending it via Gmail is not as secure as it seems. Zip files are notoriously easy to crack; ditto for MS Word passwords.

Instead, go to Firefox Send at https://send.firefox.com. This site is hosted by Mozilla – yup, the Thunderbird and Firefox folks. You can just drag and drop your file onto this site and it will encrypt it and then create a link that automatically expires. You can add as many files as you want up to a totla of 1GB. You can do all of this without signing in or creating an account. If you do sign-in, however, you can add up to 2.5GB of files.

One Hundred Years of Solitude Family Tree.pdf
1.1MB
X

The Odyssey Notes.docx
804.8KB
X

(+) Select files to upload   Total size: 1.9MB

Expires after 1 download ⌄ or 1 day ⌄

🔒 Protect with password ••••••

Upload

In addition, you can choose to expire this link after 1 to 100 downloads, or 5 minutes to 1 week of time; whichever comes first. Changing either of these parameters requires a login, otherwise, it will default to 1-day or 1 download. You can also, optionally, protect the download with a password.

After you click Upload, it will generate a link which you can copy and email to the recipient (e.g. your accountant in this scenario). As you can see this link is non-guessable, so the odds that anyone will accidentally stumble upon it are essentially zero.

Your file is encrypted and ready to send

Copy the link to share your file:

Send-Archive.zip

https://send.firefox.com/download/05168dd30d9bdf09/#eCc

Copy link

OK

So when the recipient gets this link and they click on it, they will first have to enter a password if you entered one, otherwise it will bring them to a page to download the files. Once the files are downloaded the link will expire.

Another similar service to Firefox send is Let's Upload That File by Disroot. This will allow a link to remain active for up to 30 days if needed. The total file size is up to 1GB.

UPDATE: Firefox Send has been suspended due to abuse by issuers of malware. The best alternative as of this writing is FileMail at https://www.filemail.com/. You can send 5GB files for free which remain on the site for 7 days. Paid options are available.

Sharing Information Securely with PrivateBin

Let's say you want to send a piece of information -- not a file-- but text, to someone. This might be a password for the tax file in the above scenario. Or maybe you want to send your spouse the new password to the banking site since they made you change it when you logged in.

This is where PrivateBin comes in handy. You can enter any text you want and choose the expiration time for the link (from 5 minutes to 1 year) or choose 'Never'. There is also a 'Burn after reading' checkbox which will remove the data as soon as the first person reads it. If you do not select this box, the data will remain until the expiration time.

When you hit Send it will generate a long link that you share with whoever you need to see the information. You can text it to them or email it. Since PrivateBin has a mobile app, the receiver can view the information directly on their phone.

Another nice feature is instead of *Burn After Reading*, you can choose 'Open Discussion'. This allows you to have a secure text conversation with one or more parties. You can share information back and forth until the expiration time, after which the entire conversation will be deleted forever.

Chapter 14 - Home Networking...Safely

Your home network probably consists of the router that was provided to you by the ISP (e.g. Verizon, Comcast, Time-Warner, Cox, Optimum, etc.) which typically includes a wireless access point as well. If you have a small business then you may have a small switch/router combination in addition to the box the ISP setup.

There are two points of access that need to be secure to prevent unknown persons from accessing your home network:(1) the router itself; and (2) the wireless network.

Your Home Router

The first order of business is to prevent anyone on the Internet from accessing your router. If they do gain access to the router there are many exploits that can be used to which may make your router part of a DDoS attack, or reroute your access to certain websites to malicious sites, plus a myriad of other security issues. The most important thing to prevent this is to ensure that the firewall is turned on for your router. This should be the default in nearly all cases. Another important item is to disable remote access (aka remote management) to the router. Whether this is on or off by default depends on the manufacturer. The commands to perform this action is different for each model but you can search for it on the Internet. The third critical action is to change the password that

came with our router. This is especially true if you
need to leave the remote management enabled. It is
extremely easy for someone on the Internet to
determine what type of router you have and then
lookup the default login. This then gives them direct
access to your home networking device. If you don't
believe it is easy to get this information, take a peek
at Default Router Passwords and
RouterPasswords.com.

Next is the Wi-Fi feature -- just about every router
now has this capability built-in. In some cases you
may have a wireless access point connected to the
router via a wired connection. Either way, there are
two important settings that need to be enabled. First,
do not use open access on your Wi-Fi! Change the
password to something other than the default. Letting
your Wi-Fi be accessible without a password will
allow neighbors and passers-by full access to the
internet at your expense. If they were to do something
that illegal while connected, it will look like it came
from your address. In addition, once on your local
network it makes hacking into your connected
devices easy enough for even the newest script
kiddie. Anyone connected to your Wi-Fi could just
download WireShark and capture all of your data
(like websites you visit and your login information).
All of these tips are even more critical if you live in a

condo or apartment building where many people live within Wi-Fi range of each other.

When setting up the Wi-Fi network there is typically a choice of security protocols. If you have an older device it will only have WEP. If that is the case, please upgrade immediately. WEP can be cracked by anyone using aircrack-ng in less than 10 minutes. Set your security protocol to WPA2 + AES. In addition, most routers have WPS enabled by default. This is typically a button that makes it easy to add new devices to an existing network without entering long passphrases. This can be useful when setting up a printer or other device that needs to associate with the router. However, there are several security flaws in this protocol that can allow unauthorized devices to attach to your network. Once you have your network set up and everything connected to the Wi-Fi, go back and disable WPS.

The network name that broadcasts from the access point so you can find your network is called the SSID. Hiding the SSID can make it difficult to set up and connect devices and is likely not necessary, however changing the SSID name is a good practice. The default name is dependent upon the vendor. Ideally, you do not want to advertise your equipment manufacturer, your address, or your name. Something generic is best, but anything that cannot easily be associated with you or where you live; and yes people know the names of their neighbors' pets, so that should be avoided as well. Here are some examples of SSID names to avoid:

123JacksonSt.

TheJoneses

Apt156

RiversideDr

RogersHouse

Many routers also have a second guest network available. If you have guests come over frequently (friends, family members, or visitors to your small business office) you should give them access to this and avoid giving out your main network passcode. Do not connect any devices to this guest network. This will separate out data traffic between you and your guests.

In summary here is a home router and access point security checklist:

Enable firewall

Disable remote management

Change administrator default password

Ensure WPA2 enabled for Wi-Fi

Add strong password to Wi-Fi

Turn off WPS

Change your DNS settings (see below)

One final tip on home networking and Wi-Fi: if you are able to connect a device via Ethernet wire, you should do it. I know that wires can look messy, but most of the time they can be hidden. Your internet speed will be better in most cases, and it is one less device available to be scanned via Wi-Fi.

Other Home Networking Tips

Firewalls: It is best practice to enable the firewall for each of your devices connected to the network. While the firewall in the router provides the bulk of the protection to the network as a whole, the local device firewalls add an extra layer. This is handy if a device on the local network gets infected and tries to propagate itself to every local device; ransomware is notorious for this tactic.

DNS: Every website is accessed via a numerical IP address. Since numbers are hard to remember the Domain Name Service (DNS) translates these numerical IP addresses into readable names we can remember (e.g. cnn.com). All ISPs offer their own DNS service when you purchase internet service, and typically it is programmed into the router by default. There are three problems with using the default ISP DNS addresses.

> *Performance*: Many ISPs do not have large distributed DNS servers in different areas of the country; sometimes they just have a primary and secondary and all of their

customers use the same server. This can drag web performance down during busy times.

Safety: As it has been noted previously there are many websites that have been compromised and disseminate malware when you visit them. Most ISPs do not have the staff to block these sites, let alone track and verify the reported information. This leaves you vulnerable.

Privacy: Your ISP can see every website you request in your browser, even if you are using HTTPS, even if you have a VPN. Since you always start a session by typing a website name in your browser, it must then go to their DNS servers for address translation. Now that Net Neutrality is dead, your ISP is definitely keeping tabs on where you are visiting in order to use this data for resale. In addition, they could decide to throttle your bandwidth based on the site you visit. Maybe Netflix lost a bidding war to Disney with your ISP, so Netflix is slow compared to Disney channel -- this is now a real possibility without Net Neutrality.

Do not despair! There is a solution. If you want to increase your internet performance, protect your PCs from malicious sites, and keep your ISP from knowing which sites you visit -- and thereby prevent data throttling-- you need to change your DNS settings to a third-party. Luckily, there are several good secure DNS services available that are absolutely free. Making this change can be done on a per device level, however, it is best to change it on your router so that every device will automatically be protected when it gets an address from the router.

In your WAN settings on your router there will be a setting to enter 2 (sometimes 3) DNS Server addresses. You will likely see the ISP server addresses there already. You should replace these with one of the secure services below:

Quad-9 (9.9.9.9)
CloudFlare (1.1.1.1)
OpenDNS (208.67.222.222)

Visit each of these sites to get specific instructions on how to configure your home router to use their service. I recommend Quad-9; they have very fast servers, and they quickly update their DNS to redirect you to safety for known infected sites. Consider changing your DNS setting a 'must-do'.

Chapter 15 - Using a VPN

A VPN, or virtual private network, is software used to secure an internet connection. It ensures that the data in transmission (i.e. sending and receiving) is encrypted, preventing others from snooping on your traffic. This is protection provided above and beyond any websites that are SSL (https) encrypted. It will also pertain to chat data, file transfers, uploading photos to Facebook, and all internet activity. The VPN provider's software will encrypt the data and then reroute your data through their servers. At this point the data is decrypted and sent to the final destination.

What are some important uses for VPNs?
Public Wi-Fi protection

Never use public Wi-Fi without enabling a VPN! If you work a lot in coffee shops, hotels, and other places that provide free Internet access - it is very simple for anyone else on the network to use Wireshark and sniff out all your transaction data. Outside of your home network, always use a VPN for your own protection.

Accessing local data from outside your home area

If you travel overseas and try to access NetFlix -- for example-- you will see that you are not allowed due to license restrictions. This is the same music sites, streaming TV, and many entertainments sites. There are even some countries that block specific content. Using a VPN makes it seem like you are somewhere else. You could be in London, and by connecting to your VPN you appear to be in Chicago, which means you are now able to rot your brain with The Bachelor and America's Got Talent instead of whatever they have in Britain...okay, maybe this is not a good example, but you get the point.

Prevent your ISP from collecting data on which websites you visit.

Your VPN should provide DNS servers and proxy all of your traffic through their encrypted tunnel, so your ISP cannot see or collect any data about which sites you are visiting. As was stated before, this is important without Net Neutrality so that if they decide to throttle the bandwidth for a site that you visit regularly, this will not pertain to you since the ISP is unaware that you are visiting the site.

Hide your IP Address

When you use a VPN connection you get a new IP address that belongs to the provider. This means others cannot trace your connection back to your home location.

All VPN providers are not alike.

There are dozens (hundreds?) of VPN providers available today. The problem is that many of them do not provide real privacy. They may leak your DNS queries to your ISP, which means your data can still be harvested and your bandwidth can be throttled. Some are small and only have a few servers in several locations which means that you may experience sluggish connections. Also, many log your real IP address and keep track of which sites you visit. This data can then be resold -- thereby moving the problem from your ISP to the VPN provider.

Here is the first rule for VPNs -- do not use any VPN that is free. You might think it is great to get something for free, but once again, this makes your data their business model. The free provider typically have slow connections and/or limit your total data. Other tactics to make money include the capture and resell of your data or put pop-up ads in your face every time you change websites. This makes for a very frustrating experience and then you will likely stop using the VPN altogether.

So if you're going to purchase an annual plan for a VPN provider, what criteria should you for in a provider? Here are a few factors other than price:
> Allow access from multiple devices across platforms such as Windows, Mac, Android, iPhone, etc.
> Do not log your IP address or any information about your web activity
> Have many servers (hundreds) in many countries around the globe
> Free trial and 30+ day cancellation policy
> Good connection speeds
> DNS leak protection

Internet Kill Switch
>(This will disconnect you from the internet if your VPN goes down)

After signing-up for the service, install the VPN software and do the following checks:
>Go to whatismyip.com and note your IP address and location.
>Enable the VPN and refresh the https://www.whatismyip.com/ page and ensure that the IP address and location have changed.
>Now go to speedtest.net and see that you get reasonably good connection speeds.
>Now check that you are not leaking DNS by going to http://dnsleak.com and running the test in your browser.
>Use the VPN for your normal internet activity for a week and change servers occasionally to make sure that the other servers also perform well.

Here are some recommended VPN providers that check all the boxes.

The best bet is to do a search online for the best VPN provider and the current year and after selecting one, compare it against the criteria above. However, the companies below are already known to be fast, reliable, private, and relatively inexpensive.

NordVPN -- This is my favorite provider and I have used them for years. They have lots of servers all over the world, there is zero logging of data, and you will get a fast internet connection. Nord is based in Panama, and their pricing plans are between $3 - $7 per month. There's a NordVPN application for Windows, macOS, Linux, plus apps for iOS, Android, and Android TV. Also there are encrypted extensions for Chrome and Firefox. You can connect up to 6 devices with your paid plan. They have discounts for students and non-profits as well -- check the site for pricing.

Another favorite is ProtonVPN. This Swiss company is the same that offers ProtonMail (see Chapter 5) and focused on user privacy. They have over 351 servers in 31 countries at this writing. Pricing for paid plans is between $4 and $24 per month. You can connect up to 6 devices. Also, they offer a free version which lets you connect 1 device from up to 3 countries. The network speed for the free version is slow. This is an exception to the above rule about never use free; Proton set this up to aid journalists to access their email and files privately from around the world. They extend this service to the public as well. This is a great way to test out a VPN, or if you need one in a pinch and still don't have one. If you like the service, get the paid version for a better online experience.

Another good site is OVPN. They are based out of Sweden and their pricing plans are around $7 - $11 per month. They also support Windows, macOS, Linux, plus apps for iOS, Android, and a host of other operating systems and hardware devices. This is especially a great option if you are based in Europe.

Chapter 16 - Keeping Your Physical Space Safe

In this chapter we will discuss keeping your PC and data secure in a physical space where others may be nearby. Also, we address keeping your camera and microphone secure to prevent spying. While you may think this is paranoid, there are websites that when visited can hijack your camera or mic without your knowledge. There have been cases where a person brought their PC into a repair shop, and later found that spying software allowed others to view the person through the webcam without even the LED light alerting them. Additionally, there is a known flaw in Chrome browser that can make this even easier for hijackers (are you still using Chrome?!) Let's start with the camera since this is the easiest device to secure. If you don't use it much or at all, you can put a piece of electrical tape over it. Even Mark Zuckerberg and former FBI Director James Comey both put tape over their computer's camera when not in use. If you tend to use your camera often for conferencing and taking beautiful selfies of your latest makeover then you may need a sliding webcam cover. They sell them online in packs of 3 or more for about $10. These let you alternately hide and expose the camera lens on your PC. If you have a USB camera, simply unplug it when not in use. Another method for preventing unauthorized camera access on Windows 10 is to go to Settings >> Privacy >> Camera and at the top of the page, you will see the option to let apps use my camera. Toggle the slider to the left to turn camera access off for all apps.

Securing the microphone is a bit trickier. The easiest way to do this is to find an old pair of earbuds -- you know the one you've been meaning to throw away but figured they could be used for something, well you were right! Cut the 3.5mm jack off of the earbuds as close to the connector as possible. If you were stick this into the PC audio jack, it would now effectively disable the microphone because your PC thinks there is an external mic attached -- but there is no way for the audio to be input. When you want to use your built-in mic just unplug it. It's that simple.

One final thing that should be obvious but I have to mention because so many people do this - and you know who you are... Do not write down passwords on paper or sticky notes and post them on your PC, your bulletin board, or even inside your desk drawer. Now that you are using a password manager (you are right?) this should not be necessary anyway. This is especially important at work since you do not always have control over your physical space. If you were crazy enough to use the same password at work as you do for your personal stuff, then you are really taking chances.

If you do want to store your passwords on paper for safe keeping, then keep them in a safe. Seriously. Once a year I export all of my passwords from LastPass and print them onto paper. I then store this paper in my fireproof safe. I then shred the downloaded password file using File Shredder.

Working in Cafes and Shared Spaces

If you spend a lot of time away from home and like to work in coffee shops, restaurants, hotels or the public library then this section will be even more relevant for you. We already mentioned that the first rule of security in these scenarios is to always use a VPN. There are a few other things that can keep your data and online activities private.

First of all, as mentioned above, hopefully you do not have any passwords lying around on scraps of paper, folders, or sticky noted to your screen!

Secondly, these work areas also tend to be crowded with people sitting closely next to you, or behind you and constantly walking passed your PC screen. A good investment for around $30 is a laptop privacy screen filter. You can find many of these on Amazon; you just need to get one that is the same size as your screen. The filters blackout your screen when viewing from the side, but maintain a crystal clear view straight-on. Many also protect your eyes from glare, UV, and blue light. So unless someone is directly over your shoulder they will not be able to see what is on your screen. They are easily removable for when you need to show others something on your PC.

The next area of concern when in close proximity to others is Bluetooth devices. Most PCs support Bluetooth for a mouse, speaker, keyboard, and other peripherals. One Microsoft feature called Swift Pair pairs and connects Bluetooth compatible devices almost instantly by detecting them when they're in close proximity to your Windows 10 computer. This is a great convenience for you, and a security hazard when out and about. If you have Bluetooth discoverability on -- usually true by default-- then other devices can see your Bluetooth address, which makes pairing attempts much easier. Pairing a device usually requires entering a PIN but not always. Once someone nearby is paired with your PC, all kinds of information can be collected including access to files and tracking your key presses. Here are some important Bluetooth safety guidelines:

Enable Bluetooth functionality only when needed.

Enable Bluetooth discovery only when necessary.

Keep paired devices close together and monitor what is happening on the devices.

Never enter passkeys or PINs when unexpectedly prompted to do so.

Regularly update and patch Bluetooth-enabled devices.

Remove paired devices immediately after use

You can get to your Bluetooth settings on a Mac by Apple menu --> System Preferences.
You can get to them on Windows via Control Panel.

Another security issue to be aware of for Microsoft is Network discovery. This allows Windows to find other computers and devices on a network. This feature is on by default for private networks like the one in your home or workplace. Network discovery is turned off by default for public networks. This is what you want. However, if your network is not defined as Public or if you changed the settings for network discovery, then everyone else with a Windows PC can find and attempt to connect to your PC.

You can double-check this in Windows 10 by going to Settings - Network & Internet - Wi-Fi then click Change Advanced Sharing Settings. Find and expand the current profile. Look at the Network discover section and ensure that it is off for Public (or all) networks.

A final word on the ubiquitous USB Flash drive. They are very convenient, cheap, and easy to carry around. However, USB drives can contain malware -- especially if it was in another person's PC that was infected-- or they could have trojans that can compromise your PC. If these drives have a file called 'autorun.inf' it can infect your computer before you have a chance to even format the drive. While modern versions of Windows and Mac no longer run programs on a USB stick by default, other attacks can make a USB drive appear to be something else, such as a keyboard, and then be used to take malicious actions. Honestly the best way to prevent problems is to only use USB flash drives that you bought personally and came in original packaging. If you have a good AntiVirus program running then some of these also catch infections on USB drives before they can cause damage - but check on the vendor's web page or contact support.

Chapter 17 - The Internet of (Dangerous) Things, aka IoT

The fastest growth in consumer electronics is with interconnected devices using IP addresses that are categorically known as the "Internet of Things (IOT)". This includes Nest thermostats, Ring doorbells, security cameras, LED light bulbs, garage door openers, gaming consoles, refrigerators, Smart TVs, and soon a whole slew of new devices. There will soon be a half a billion IoT devices in the USA alone and they are vulnerable and present a growing cyber threat. In order to get these products to market quickly there has been a serious lack of concern regarding security--especially since there is no penalty for the manufacturer. If someone hacks into your PC via your online fish tank and steals your passwords and accounts, you have no recourse with the vendor. (Don't laugh, this exact scenario happened to a casino.)

The sheer lack of security features in most IoT devices can allow for exploitation on a large scale. The Mirai virus emerged in 2016 and launched a massive DDoS attack by taking control of people's home devices like printers and baby monitors. Security pros have shown how everyday systems like a connected television can be hacked, and once bad actors are into your IoT system, they can gain access to the network and other devices.

Alexa and Google Home

Security experts recently have found ways to hack into and control these speakers' voice assistants with methods including undetectable audio commands, voice squatting attacks, and eavesdropping software. This is even more problematic now that many new Echo devices include a camera. The drop-in feature is a privacy invasion waiting to happen. Drop-In allows you to video call a trusted friend without them needing to confirm the call. If you enable drop-In for a certain user, calling them will allow you to start seeing video from their Echo after a few seconds of warning. I don't know if this has been exploited yet, but once there is a backdoor or hack found you can be sure there will be voyeurism on a large scale in hacker-land.

You can use the same fundamental protection methods we have been discussing the whole book (see below for another reminder). Additionally, if you have one of these voice-based personal assistants, it is a good practice to change the "wake word" if possible. Choose something that is rarely if ever spoken and does not sound too much like another word. You are trying to prevent accidental activation in which case the device starts recording and saving everything it hears. This will also prevent your friends from playing practical jokes when you are not in the room: "Hey Alexa, set a 3am alarm with horror movie sounds!"

There are some home-based products now coming onto the market place to help detect when someone hacks into a device on your network and attempt to shut it down before any damage is done. One of these devices is the Bitdefender Box2 but there are others as well. These devices provide security features such as vulnerability assessment, content filtering, exploit prevention, anomaly detection, and phishing prevention. There is typically an annual fee for these devices in addition to the cost of the device.

There are some basic precautions that can be taken to prevent hacking of IoT devices. Most of these tips are similar to the advice given in other chapters, but there is a reason for that -- this advice works and is important.

The first action is to decide, do you really need the device? Yes, it's cool to have the latest technology, even if you never realized that you "needed" it, but technology for technology-sake can get you into trouble. Do you need to be able to turn on the light in your house from your phone? I am still not convinced anyone needs a refrigerator connected to the internet, but, these things are coming one way or the other. Many Smart TVs won't even perform a setup without being connected to the Internet. My only point here, is be strategic in connecting devices to your home network, only use something that will really benefit you.

Next, make sure you change all default settings, especially the password. Use the same guidelines as discussed previously when creating a password. If there are privacy settings for your device, check them out and turn on whatever makes sense. If your device can have a name, be careful how you name it -- there's no point in giving out clues to what is connected to your network.

Not all IoT devices have a mechanism for updating their software or firmware. This means it will be obsolete sooner than later and try to avoid purchasing such a product. If your IoT device can do updates, make sure that you update as soon as you can since most of these updates include security upgrades.

Finally, if you rarely use a device, or if you are leaving home for more than a few days, disconnect or power down all IoT devices. It is even advisable to disable your home Wi-Fi if you go on vacation. The less things connected to your network at any given time provides less points of forced entry into the network.

If your router has a Guest Wi-Fi connection and you don't really use it -- i.e., you don't have any friends or family, or maybe they don't visit and you like it that way -- you could turn that guest network into a separate IoT network. Connect all of the smart devices in your home onto this network and keep your PCs and personal data on the main Wi-Fi network. This will provide some separation if someone does hack in or one of the IoT devices fails and starts spewing bad packets all over the place.

Chapter 18 - If You Do Nothing Else...

If after reading all of the above chapters and I still haven't convinced you that the online world can be more dangerous than telling your Italian mother that her meatballs need more spice, then I am not sure why you kept reading. But since you did, and if you want the absolute minimal effort in protecting your data and computing devices then here are just two things you should do:

Perform Backups

You should perform regular backups of all your important files. Ideally, this should include a local copy and a cloud copy. Keep a USB drive connected to your PC at all times and run a daily sync to this drive for local safekeeping. Use a backup solution like

Backblaze to ensure your files against ransomware and the loss of your physical computer and USB drive (drive failure, theft, fire, etc.). Do it today!

Complete all System Updates

Regardless of which operating system or device you are using, when the manufacturer sends out updates to the hardware (e.g. BIOS) or the operating system, perform the patch as soon as possible. Many people are afraid to complete updates because they do not want to reboot and also they believe that it will break much of their software. In reality this could happen, but it occurs much less often than in the past. If it were to happen the vendors of the other product generally have a fix in place in a matter of days. In general this should almost never happen, and the added protection is worth it. Most updates to operating systems are not features, but bug fixes and security patches. Apply the updates!

After doing the above two actions, hopefully you will go back and implement some of the other critical activities in this book. If I had to come up with another list of the most important, it would probably change on any given day, but for today, that list would be:

Start using a password manager (e.g. BitWarden)

Change the password on all of your financial, social, and email sites to a unique and long password

Use Two-Factor authentication on the above sites where provided

Purchase and use a VPN

Put a password on your home Wi-Fi if you don't already have one

Change the default password on any internet connected device

Thanks for reading and stay safe online!

Appendix - Additional Resources

If you are interested in learning more about how to protect all of your online devices and the latest threats to your data, or just to keep up with the latest data breaches...here are a few good resources:

Krebs on Security, blog:
https://krebsonsecurity.com/

Bruce Schneier on Security, blog:
https://www.schneier.com/

The Electronic Frontier Foundation:
https://www.eff.org/
"The leading nonprofit defending digital privacy, free speech, and innovation."
Check out the Tools section of the website.

Online Security Checklist, https://securitycheckli.st/
"An open source checklist of resources designed to improve your online privacy and security."

PrivacyTools.io at https://www.privacytools.io
My go-to list for everything and anything related to privacy and data security. Many of these tools were featured in this book.

Made in the USA
Middletown, DE
10 September 2021

48048796R00087